Transforming Learning Through Tangible Instruction

Transforming Learning Through Tangible Instruction offers a transformative, student-centered approach to higher education pedagogy that integrates embodied cognition into classroom practice. Evidence across disciplines makes clear that people learn with their bodies as well as their brains, but no previous book has provided evidence-based guidance for adopting and refining its practice in colleges and universities. Collecting findings from cognitive science, educational neuroscience, learning theories, and beyond, this volume's unique approach—radical yet practical, effective yet low-cost—will have profound implications for higher education faculty and administrators engaged in teaching and learning. Seven concise chapters explore how physical objects, hands-on making, active construction, and other elements of body and environment can enhance comprehension, memory, and individual and collaborative learning.

Sarah Kuhn is Professor Emerita in the Department of Psychology at the University of Massachusetts Lowell, USA. Before beginning her thirty-year teaching career, she received a PhD in Urban Studies and Planning from the Massachusetts Institute of Technology and a Bachelor of Arts in Philosophy and Social Psychology from Harvard University. She is the author of numerous articles, including several on aspects of learning with things in interdisciplinary, studio-based, and community settings.

Transforming Learning Through Tangible Instruction

The Case for Thinking With Things

SARAH KUHN

Routledge
Taylor & Francis Group
NEW YORK AND LONDON

First published 2022
by Routledge
605 Third Avenue, New York, NY 10158

and by Routledge
2 Park Square, Milton Park, Abingdon, Oxon, OX14 4RN

Routledge is an imprint of the Taylor & Francis Group, an informa business

Library of Congress Cataloging-in-Publication Data
Names: Kuhn, Sarah, author.
Title: Transforming learning through tangible instruction : the case for thinking with things / by Sarah Kuhn.
Description: New York, NY : Routledge, 2021. | Includes bibliographical references and index. |
Identifiers: LCCN 2021015671 (print) | LCCN 2021015672 (ebook) | ISBN 9780367652708 (hardback) | ISBN 9780367653538 (paperback) | ISBN 9781003129073 (ebook)
Subjects: LCSH: College teaching. | Active learning. | Human body in education. | Student-centered learning. | Cognitive neuroscience.
Classification: LCC LB2331 .K84 2021 (print) | LCC LB2331 (ebook) | DDC 378.1/25—dc23
LC record available at https://lccn.loc.gov/2021015671
LC ebook record available at https://lccn.loc.gov/2021015672

ISBN: 978-0-367-65270-8 (hbk)
ISBN: 978-0-367-65353-8 (pbk)
ISBN: 978-1-003-12907-3 (ebk)

Typeset in Bembo and Avenir
by Apex CoVantage, LLC

To my Teachers
(in order of appearance)

Kay and Tom

Liza and Nat

Don and Ben

Ralph and Jane

Emma and Sam

Contents

Figures

Acknowledgments

In a sense, this work has been underway since I first built structures with wooden blocks in my childhood playroom. I have incurred a lifetime of debts along the way. I am deeply grateful to all of you, named and unnamed.

For important and sustained conversations over the years, I want to thank Jeanne Bamberger, Mary Catherine Bateson, Diana Coluntino, Bruce Corson, Judith Davidson, Ron Eglash, Ann Enkoji, Mitchell Kapor, Fred Martin, Lise Motherwell, Robert Rasmussen, Ellen Schön, Carol Strohecker, and Sherry Turkle.

I am also grateful to many who showed their enthusiasm for this project through conversations, invitations to present, feedback, and other forms of support. I want to particularly mention Marsha Brofka-Berends, Scott Bultman, Dale Dougherty, Elizabeth Branch Dyson, Chris Hansen, Mark Johnson, Sheila Kirschbaum, David Kuhn, Jehane Kuhn, Judy Kuhn, Robert Kunzendorf, June Lemen, Caitrin Lynch, Alex Ruthmann, Kristina Lamour Sansone, John Schumacher, Barbara Walker, and John Wooding.

Several groups were also important to the formation of my ideas: the Thinking With Things Faculty Learning Community; the Center for Women and Work Faculty Associates; and the members of the Lowell Tex project, all at the University of Massachusetts Lowell, as well as the participants in Conversing with Materials conversations.

Critical support came from the National Science Foundation EAGER grant (Award # IIS-1042580) and Mary Lou Maher, and from sabbaticals spent at the Radcliffe Institute for Advanced Study and the Franklin W. Olin College of Engineering.

Thanks to Daniel Schwartz at Routledge, the editor any author would be fortunate to have, and to two anonymous reviewers.

For sustaining me on the very long road that has been this book, I am deeply grateful to Sarah Fletcher, Jack Grady, Karen Hampton, Jane Kite, Liza Kuhn, Nat Kuhn, Ralph LaChance, Barbara Lipski, Evelyn Smith Scally, Astrig Tanguay, Amy Totenberg, and my wonderful children, Emma and Sam LaChance. My writing accountability group—Marlowe Miller and Judith Davidson—have been especially important in giving me strength for the journey.

Finally, I want to thank my students, from whom I have learned so much.

1 Unnatural Acts: The Problem With What We Do Now

I'd like to invite you into a classroom, a typical room at my typical university. I've been teaching for more than 25 years and have used scores of different classrooms around our campus; almost all of them are like the one I'm about to show you.

Your first impression will be of beige. Beige chairs with a single broad arm for notebooks, all facing the teacher's spot at the front of the room. Beige tile flooring, beige walls with nothing much on them except the requisite whiteboard on one wall—or two walls if I am lucky. A wooden podium in front has a bunch of electronic gear so I can show PowerPoint slides, or an image from the web, or a video on the white pull down screen. Even the digital projector fastened to the ceiling is tan against the off-white acoustical tile. There are green trees outside the window, but the beige blinds are usually pulled down so that I can use the projector without competition from daylight.

The classroom I've described is so common on campuses today that it hardly rates a mention. It's standard issue, and so is the way of teaching that it supports. Almost any student in America, walking into this room, will immediately know what is expected of them: sit down, take out your notebook, and wait for the professor to begin. Likewise, this room tells me, the professor, what is expected of me. I am to be the center of attention, up front at my podium, and all the learning that happens in this space will be dispensed by me. The tools I have at my disposal are a whiteboard and a

Figure 1.1 One of many similar classrooms to which the author has been assigned.

computer for projecting images. The students have their notebooks. Why would we need anything more?

Over my three decades of teaching, this standard arrangement, which I once took for granted, has come to seem to me deeply problematic. It's not that students don't learn in these classrooms—they do—but they often learn in spite of, not because of, the standard arrangement. It's as if we were asking them to go into battle with (almost literally, as I shall show) their hands tied.

Like most new professors, I started my teaching career with little teaching experience and completely unaware of the research on what works to promote learning in college students. I made many, many mistakes. I also learned from some of those mistakes, and from students, colleagues, and staff at my university, and began to try new ways of approaching lessons. Emboldened by a semester I spent observing a studio classroom in a school of architecture, I introduced small hands-on exercises in my social science classes. The first time I brought a bucket of Lego bricks to my undergraduates, they were both thrilled and baffled. I asked them to make a quick "sketch model" of an environmentally sustainable community—that week's subject—by arranging the Lego pieces on a tabletop in the classroom. The students' alert engagement, their happy conversation as they used the Lego, their interesting accounts of what they had chosen to build, and their clear inability to apply any of the lessons of sustainability I'd been trying to teach them, all set me upon a path of inquiry that continues to this day.

My Lego experience led to many other uses of hands-on materials in the classroom: having students, on the first day of class, spend five minutes building a Lego structure that expresses something about how they like to learn; using poster paper to have groups of students make and present quick in-class posters about a topic related to that week's subject matter; using Tinkertoys to create collaborative "concept maps" that reveal the relationships within a set of ideas; and modeling the structures of the brain with clay to bring the image off the page and into three dimensions. These and other forays into terrain far beyond the standard model of classroom behavior have been a wonderful adventure for me and (for the most part) for my students. The success and the pure fun of these adventures led me to create a "studio classroom" for myself and my colleagues, full of hands-on materials and resources.

The studio classroom began a decade-and-a-half ago when, with support from the university, I converted a derelict storage room into a teaching space with work tables, craft materials, simple electronics, project storage, networked computers, and a few other resources. When I teach in this space, students are more engaged and relaxed. Student reflections written at the end of a semester in the studio classroom reflect this and its positive impact on learning:

> I liked the hands on learning approach. It breaks up the constant barrage of regular classes. It did meet my learning needs because I learn better through hands on.

> I do not learn well in a lecture structured course. I work better with my hands and physically seeing and doing what we are discussing. . . . Not only did you teach us about the information, we then got to physically do some kind of activity to help really understand what we were being taught.

> This class used various different teaching methods and I thought that this variety was very successful and helped me greatly in learning the materials. . . . I liked this because it is something that is not usual in classrooms but I know it helped me and I think it helped other students to learn because the atmosphere was more relaxed.

> I definitely did not expect that on the first day of class we would be tying knots, or that our first homework assignment would be to learn to crochet, but it was a great experience nonetheless. . . . I have never taken a class with so much hands-on learning, or student centered teaching. . . . One of the things I liked best about this course was the room in which the course took place . . . it felt like a little learning community.

> The way for me to learn is to interact. I tend to fall asleep if I am just listening or watching so it helped me stay interested in the class. The course could be improved if it also tended to our taste as well. Just kidding.

> I am confident in saying that I will retain more information from this class than any other class I took this semester.

While these students were particularly articulate, their comments are representative of the feedback I got every semester. It's responses like these that made me realize that my hands-on, thinking-with-things approach spoke to students in a deep and resonant way that was important to pursue. Ultimately, it was the reactions of students, and the satisfaction and pleasure I found in the new studio classroom, that led me to write this book.

What happens in my new classroom is far enough from the mainstream that I now begin each semester by talking explicitly with my students about my approach and its rationale. On the first day of class, I pass out a list I call "Five Myths About Learning in College." I want them to understand why I do the unconventional things that I do, and to know that this will not be the passive classroom they may have expected.

Five Myths About Learning in College

Myth 1: Learning takes place inside our heads, so the rest of our body should remain still except to take notes.

Myth 2: College learning is about learning facts, and all you need to learn facts is lectures and textbooks.

Myth 3: "Experiential Learning" requires going off campus—to study abroad, do service learning, or do a co-op placement.

Myth 4: College students are abstract thinkers and have no problem learning new things when they are presented abstractly.

Myth 5: If you have trouble learning in college it means there is something wrong with you.

In the pages that follow, I will address these myths and many other assumptions, spoken and unspoken, that guide most pedagogy in higher education today. By presenting evidence from research and from my own experience and that of others who teach college students, I hope to convince you, the reader, to replace these myths with a more effective, generative set of beliefs grounded in how we truly learn.

Coming Attractions

As a preview of coming attractions, here is a brief sketch of the ground I will cover in the upcoming chapters of this book:

A foundational assumption of conventional approaches to college teaching is the distinction between mind and body, evident in such phrases as "the life of the mind"—the promotion of which is the presumptive focus of the university. Going back at least to the 17th century philosopher Descartes, the mind/body distinction has guided approaches to learning in Western thought. As a result, although institutions of higher education may offer athletic and exercise programs, they are extra-curricular, and the focus is on the development of students' minds, thought to be synonymous with the contents of their heads.

Thanks to the work of psychologists, neuroscientists, philosophers, and others, one of the key things we now know about human learning is that it is *embodied*; that is, that our hands, our bodies, our sense of ourselves in space and in motion, all play an important and inadequately understood role not only in our learning, but also in our thinking. This is the subject of Chapter 2, "The Embodied Learner." Drawing on the work of philosopher John Dewey, psychologist Rudolf Arnheim, neuroscientist Antonio Damasio, and others, the compelling case for embodied cognition is laid out.

Embodied learning also means that, as John Dewey argued in the first half of the 20th century, all learning is also *experiential*: where good and deep learning are present, they grow from experience and action. In higher education, the term "experiential learning" is generally used to refer to programs that take students out into the "real world" for activities like study abroad, internships or co-ops, and service-learning. I argue that the distinction between classroom learning and experiential learning is like the distinction between mind and body, which Dewey also challenged. Both of these dichotomies are harmful and problematic, and showing this is the work of this chapter.

Chapter 3, "Thinking with Things," shows that not only are cognition and learning not confined to the contents of the skull, but also that our bodies and our environment become "things to think with" that enhance comprehension, learning, and memory. Much of the chapter is an extended discussion of an historical case: the Froebel Kindergarten, which became widespread throughout Europe and North America in the second half of the 19th century. Key to the Froebel Kindergarten was a carefully designed set of manipulatives to be used by children as they created patterns of nature, science, and art. After a discussion of the Froebel approach and materials, the chapter goes on to argue for the deep impact that the system had on the adult work of modern artists (including Klee, Mondrian, Kandinsky, Albers, Braque, and architect Frank Lloyd Wright) and modern scientists (Richard Feynman, Buckminster Fuller, and brothers J. Robert and Frank Oppenheimer) in the first half of the 20th century.

Chapter 4, "How Things Shape Our Thinking," builds on the single example of the Kindergarten materials by enumerating a host of ways in which things influence and support our thinking. Beginning with the role objects play in long-term memory, as well as the way in which they support memory during work-in-progress, we then turn to the ways in which things aid categorization, support spatial reasoning, are key to interaction and inquiry, and evoke emotion. Things are foundational to meaning making and to metaphor, as well as being present, in real or imagined form, in the work of scientists and artists.

In social settings, both those of collaborative work and those of instruction, things play a role. In instruction, physical materials can aid tutoring by shaping the student experience, providing shared metaphors, and making the thinking of the learner visible to the instructor. In collaborative settings, like most workplaces, administrative "things" like standardized forms and large information systems also shape thought and action.

Chapter 5, "Abstraction Reconsidered," tackles a central assumption underlying pedagogy at the university level: that we are primarily teaching abstractions to students who are developmentally ready for abstract thinking. Drawing on work from cognitive psychology, neuroscience, philosophy, and other fields, this chapter challenges this point of view, which stems in part from a misreading of the seminal work of Jean Piaget. The conventional wisdom is that humans move through a developmental sequence as they age, progressing from the very concrete to the abstract, and that by the age of 18 or so, learners have become abstract thinkers. In fact, Piaget believed that the road to abstract thinking is not a single path, but that students' ability to think abstractly is domain dependent, and develops with experience.

An individual learner's evolution from concrete to abstract thinker, I argue, is not the evolution from child to adult, but the development from novice to expert that can happen at any time once the basic cognitive prerequisites have been met. Real facility with abstractions, I speculate, may in fact be a process of "concretion," bringing abstractions closer to the self.

In Chapter 6, "Embodiment Revisited", we return to embodied cognition and look closely at the hand as a very special case of embodied cognition and learning. Although the manual is devalued in higher education, we reinforce this value hierarchy at our peril. Starting with a discussion of the physiology of the mind-hand system, the chapter continues with a look at the wide variety of ways that the hand participates in cognition, starting with the senses and continuing with finger counting and other embodied practices of memory and learning. Low cognitive load manual activity also aids attention and reduces distraction, and physical materials have the potential to assist learning in those for whom it is especially difficult.

One of the most poignant results of our erroneous approach to college learning is that we call upon students to perform unnatural acts. Many students, through long practice, are able to get good and even excellent grades in this environment. Others suffer, enduring academic failure and reinforcing a poor self-image, because they have difficulty acting unnaturally. These students we label "disabled" and send them to receive special services and incremental accommodations that are supposed to lessen the impact of their defects. If, as many in the disability rights community argue, "disability" is a mismatch between person and environment, we are systematically creating disability in the standard-issue classroom. When, for example, we relegate the hand solely to note taking, we handicap students by removing a principal instrument of human experience and learning.

Chapter 7, "A Vibrant Learning Ecosystem," lays out a vision for a new way of teaching in the university. Acknowledging that all students are embodied learners, and that we can and should build our classrooms and pedagogy around this ground truth, I make a series of proposals for classroom design, curriculum and instructional approaches, and educational practices that can be implemented at a variety of scales. The core focus is the benefit of active, synthetic "making" in the classroom—making prototypes, making plans, making meaning. The chapter offers four explicit recommendations to teachers, administrators, policymakers, and other stakeholders in today's system of higher education. First, promote thinking with things to enhance learning; second, create conducive learning environments; third, educate for action; and fourth, take teaching and learning seriously. After expanding on each of these recommendations, the five myths about learning in college, enumerated in Chapter 1, are countered with five propositions about how best to promote student learning in higher education.

Finally, interspersed between chapters are short "Interludes," each of which profiles a particular sort of "thing to think with" in extra depth. I think of them as brief biographies or case studies of particular things or types of things and how they interact with us as we learn and as we work.

Many colleagues across the country are implementing and testing classroom innovations. A thinking-with-things approach is one among many important challenges to business-as-usual in the academy. Yet in its attention to the embodied learner, and the implications for pedagogy and for how we configure classrooms to support how students really learn, I believe this volume is unique. It calls on us to consider how we might, at reasonable cost and with the buy-in of all stakeholders, make a transition to a "thinking with things" approach to learning. This will entail educating faculty, students, parents, and others, as well as retrofitting classrooms and promoting collaboration between faculty, administrators, and staff. Faculty professional development and the development of doctoral students will be critical, because in the absence of other influences, faculty teach as we are taught.

My unorthodox ways have made me an object of interest and curiosity, and sometimes of hostility and derision, among my colleagues. This book is my attempt to marshal the research evidence and the examples to explain to them, and to you, why this strange behavior is so consequential, and how it points toward a very different way of teaching, learning, and thinking about higher education and adult learning. To my dedicated and hard-working fellow teachers, I hope this book will give you both permission and ammunition: permission to try something new, ammunition to convince the skeptics that this is important business. And for all who want to improve our system of education, I hope you too find inspiration in these pages.

Interlude A: The Crocheted Hyperbolic Plane

One of my favorite recent things to think with is the crocheted hyperbolic plane. A hyperbolic plane is a mathematical object from non-Euclidean geometry (that is, from a geometry unlike what most of us learn in school). A *crocheted* hyperbolic plane is a model of this non-Euclidean form, made with yarn and some simple crocheting.[1] When I first learned about the crocheted hyperbolic plane, I couldn't wait to get my hands on one.

In formal terms, a hyperbolic plane is a surface of constant negative curvature—the opposite of a sphere, which is a surface of constant positive curvature (and no, an inside-out sphere is still a sphere; a hyperbolic plane is something very different.) If you find it hard to imagine a surface of constant negative curvature, you are in good company. In fact, until the mid-19th century, the hyperbolic plane was thought by mathematicians to be an impossible object. Today it is accepted as possible, in part because of the work of geometers who built paper models as part of their inquiry into the characteristics of the hyperbolic plane.

The first crocheted hyperbolic plane was made by Dr. Daina Taimiņa, a theoretical computer scientist, who wondered whether a more robust model of the hyperbolic plane could be made using the skills she learned as a girl in Latvia. Her book, *Crocheting Adventures with Hyperbolic Planes*, was my introduction to what struck me as a most incongruous combination.

My relationship with math has been one of misery, from elementary school through graduate school. I passed my courses, sometimes even getting As, but my success came at a cost, and I was rarely engaged, let alone intrinsically motivated to pursue the study of math. This may explain why I was shocked, but also intrigued, by the idea that there could be an intersection between crochet and advanced mathematics. Although I was math averse and

Figure A.1 A hyperbolic plane created by the author.

Figure A.2 The same hyperbolic plane in a different pose.

had never held a crochet hook, I resolved to learn more. With the help of my local yarn store and the fiber guild that meets at MIT (really!) I started making hyperbolic planes. That was a few years ago now, and I haven't looked back. Crocheted hyperbolic planes continue to intrigue me.

These peculiar objects are remarkable for being the starting point to a very wide range of paths of inquiry.

Math Anxiety

By now I have made hundreds of crocheted hyperbolic planes. I often crochet in public places, like cafes and doctor's waiting rooms. Strangers approach me—people who are knitting or crocheting are easier to approach—and ask what I'm doing. Sometimes they also ask, what do you *do* with them? My answer, which sounds flip but is quite sincere, is that I use them to start conversations. They are very effective at this. Often people tell me their own stories about their relationship with math, and I hear a lot of tales of aversion, sorrow, and difficulty. Sometime they say, I wish math had been like this when I was in school! Making hyperbolic planes has also led me to reflect on my own relationship with math, and how much different my outlook might have been if I had crocheted my way into math, rather than having to start with the multiplication tables. In fact, I think my attitude toward math was made far worse by my formal education. It makes me think of Dewey's view that experience can be positive or negative, and of the words of a reading teacher:

> There is a way to work with a nonreading child so that by the time they finally do it, it can be almost a nonevent. . . . Or you can teach it and teach it and teach it and it's hard for them and hard for them and hard for them. And what do they learn? They learn that it's hard . . . we don't just learn what we're supposed to learn, or what the teacher believes is being taught. So I learn that I feel horrible, I learn I don't know how to do it, I learn it's difficult, I learn my mother gets angry. . . . I learn *everything*.[2]

Beauty

Crocheted hyperbolic planes are beautiful. They are sinuous, textured, malleable, and can be very colorful. I've heard people speak of the beauty of math, but assumed that I would have to be working toward a PhD (unthinkable!) in order to experience that beauty. The beauty of the planes also comes from the elegant mathematical characteristics of which they are a model. Making and sharing hyperbolic planes has given me a back door into the beauty of math; is there a way to make it the front door? Could this be a new and very different pathway to engagement with math?

Comfort and Attention

My inquiry with hyperbolic crochet, which began at the periphery of my professional interests, has insinuated itself into the core. As I crochet and as I read about these manual activities and talk with other fiber artists, I have learned that it is widely believed in the needlework community that knitting, crocheting, and stitching are relaxing, and that these activities can aid attention. Making hyperbolic planes, or just holding them, can be an antidote to math anxiety, a survival strategy for boring meetings and lectures, and good therapy for those with anxiety and attention problems.

Algorithms and Representations

A crocheted hyperbolic plane is made by starting in the center and working outward in a spiral path, repeating the same crochet stitch hundreds of times. The instructions are an algorithm, not an equation; they are of the form "make X stitches, then make two stitches in the same location." The maker can decide what X is and then follow the procedure, receiving in the process a simple introduction to algorithms and variables. A crochet pattern and a computer program would represent these same instructions in very different ways. What is the clearest way of representing this algorithm, and for what audience? How is a knitting or crochet pattern like a computer program?[3]

Emergence

Understanding the behavior of complex systems is increasing critical for our students, who must confront climate change, rapid social change and upheaval, and many other challenges of the 21st century. Emergence is a property of complex systems—the way in which something new and different can arise from a set of very simple elements—actions, organisms, or the like. The complex fractal patterns made by ice crystals on glass are an emergent phenomenon of the interaction of temperature, moisture, and material; consciousness can also be said to be an emergent property of neurons.

As you make a hyperbolic plane, its shape changes in unexpected ways. It may start as a bump or a flat disc, depending on the rate of increase and the bulkiness of the yarn. As you continue, the edges of the disc begin to buckle, then form the ruffled pattern of the finished product. Making a crocheted hyperbolic plane is a simple, tangible illustration of the systems principle of emergence, in which simple elements, repeated, form a whole that is quite unlike the individual elements.

Models

When making a hyperbolic plane, if you continue past the point where the ruffles are gentle curves, they become more acute and more tightly packed, and ultimately the crocheted hyperbolic plane approaches a sphere as its limit. The ideal, mathematical hyperbolic plane has no limit. Nor does it have thickness, or a spiral pattern. In what ways can a model both be, and not be, the thing it models? How might we be informed, or led astray, by using a model? How do the materials we choose (bulky versus thin yarn, for example) affect how the model performs?

Engagement

Crocheted hyperbolic planes are engaging, even for those who say they "hate math." I have spent hours discussing math and math education with everyone from mathematicians to math phobics since I began making and handing around these models. They draw people in and spark inquiry; they can also help people to "get a grip" on math concepts.

Notes

1. Taimiņa, D. (2018). *Crocheting adventures with hyperbolic planes: Tactile mathematics, art and craft for all to explore*. Natick, MA: CRC Press.
2. Wilson, F. (1998). *The hand: How its use shapes the brain, language, and human culture* (p. 255). New York, NY: Vintage Books.
3. For one answer, see Craig, M., Petersen, S., & Petersen, A. (2012, February). *Following a thread: Knitting patterns and program tracing*. Proceedings of the 43rd Association for Computing Machinery technical symposium on Computer Science Education, pp. 233–238. Retrieved from https://dl.acm.org/doi/10.1145/2157136.2157204.

The Embodied Learner: Thinking With the Whole Self 2

Much of what goes on in college classrooms today reflects a set of assumptions about human cognition, learning, and the nature of knowledge that are at best outmoded and at worst fundamentally wrong. We academics have a deep understanding of, and passion for, our disciplines, but we often emerge from our graduate programs knowing nothing of the research on college student learning. In fact, I already had my PhD and had been teaching for two years before I learned that there *was* research evidence on what promotes student learning in college. In the United States, you need a teaching certificate, attesting to your knowledge about how to teach, in order to teach students up to and including the 12th grade. To teach college freshmen, who are only a few months older, no training in teaching is required. The most responsible doctoral programs do make sure that their graduates receive instruction in how to teach, and many colleges have faculty development centers, but on the whole, faculty are experts in subject-matter and novices about learning. In the absence of knowledgeable guidance, we generally teach as we were taught, modeling ourselves on our admired mentors, who clearly were effective in teaching *us*. As a result, the college classroom is generally characterized by continuity, not by change. One of the results is the perpetuation of the traditional classroom and its practices, intended to mold young minds while bodies sit obediently in rows, facing forward.

Many traditions of Western thought, passed down through the centuries in our universities and infused into our culture, make a distinction between mind and body, drawing a bright line between the animalistic fallibility of the body and the senses on the one hand, and the transcendent faculties of mind and reason on the other. From the Platonists and religious teachings, through the thought of Descartes and the Enlightenment, to 20th-century schools of behaviorist psychology and artificial intelligence, the idea that mind and body are distinct has become almost an article of faith. As philosopher Mark Johnson puts it:

> Although most people never think about it very carefully, they live their lives assuming and acting according to a set of dichotomies that distinguish mind from body, reason from emotion, and thought from feeling. Mind/body dualism is so deeply embedded in our philosophical and religious traditions, in our shared conceptual systems, and in our language that it can seem to be an inescapable fact about human nature.[1]

Indeed, we are so conditioned to these distinctions that it can be very difficult to imagine how it could be otherwise.

Most of us were exposed as students to 17th-century philosopher Renee Descartes' famous aphorism, "I think, therefore I am." This classic expression of skepticism, which proceeded from Descartes' resolution to doubt everything including the evidence of his senses, spawned a long philosophical tradition that continues to this day. As an undergraduate I took a philosophy course on Descartes and skepticism and remember being introduced to the then-current problem of the "brain in the vat." For an entire semester my professor, my fellow students, and I debated whether we might be fooled into thinking that it was a chair we sat on (even if there was no chair there), or that we were in fact in the presence of other human beings with whom we were having a conversation (when it was in fact an illusion). Might we be misled by the evidence of our senses? We have all had the experience of thinking that we hear or see something that is not there; perhaps this is happening to us on a grand scale and we are pervasively and systematically deluded. Perhaps we are just brains in vats, having our neurons stimulated in ways that deceive us into thinking that we are surrounded by people and objects we naïvely believe to be real. Although this defies common sense and seems more the stuff of science fiction, we felt obliged, as serious thinkers and dedicated students of philosophy, to consider this possibility, and we strove in vain to find a way to prove that we were not in fact brains in vats, the subjects of a grand illusion. After all, it's a compelling if seemingly far-fetched story; perhaps the makers of films like *The Matrix* took a class like mine when they were in college?

Not only do we separate mind and body, we also make value judgments about the relative importance of the two. As psychologist and philosopher William James put it:

> Greek philosophers soon formed the notion that a knowledge of so-called "universals," consisting of concepts of abstract forms, qualities, numbers, and relations was the only knowledge worthy of the truly philosophic mind . . . there arose a tendency, which has lasted all through philosophy, to contrast the knowledge of universals and intelligibles, as god-like, dignified, and honorable to the knower, with that of particulars and sensibles as something relatively base which more allies us with the beasts.[2]

Nowhere in our culture today is this more true than in academia, which pledges its devotion to the transmission and creation of knowledge, reason, and the life of the mind. The elevation of reason and the intellect, and the devaluing of bodily, manual, and applied skills, show themselves in many ways: the tension between the "pure" disciplines of the humanities and mathematics, for example, and the goals, pedagogies, and practices of professional schools; the greater respect and higher status generally accorded to liberal arts education over vocational education; reverence for the theoretical over the experimental in the sciences; and the emphasis on theoretical and analytic courses rather than applied and design courses even in ultimately practical fields like engineering.

When I think of the many ways in which we favor "book smarts" over other sorts of intelligence, my mind goes back to a young woman in my Sustainable Development class. I'll call her Cathy. Until the last three weeks of the semester she was barely passing the course, and had very little to contribute to class discussions. But at the end of the course, we switched gears to focus on a quick project in which students were challenged to create an interactive device that would address some aspect of sustainable development. Like the rest of the students, Cathy and her project partner were given a handheld microprocessor that had to be incorporated into their device. To make the device interactive, students had to learn a simple programming language. Although she had no prior experience with programming, Cathy dove into the assignment and was the first in the class to have a working program. On the final day of class, at the open house where students showed their projects, I briefly sat next to Cathy during a quiet period. I complimented her on her achievement. She then confided in me that she had great trouble reading, so that she found the project phase of the class refreshing. To this day, I am both sad and angry that Cathy had not gotten the reading help she needed; I'm glad that there was something in my course that gave her the opportunity to shine. Cathy is far from unique among my students, but she is one important reason why, since that day, there has always been a project component of my courses.

The mind/body distinction and its attendant value judgments have had an impact in many fields of scholarship. The radical separation of mind and body are often accompanied by a mechanistic view of both the mind and the body, and this view is associated with schools of thought such as behaviorism in psychology (humans as stimulus-response mechanisms), objectivism in philosophy (a focus on language, propositions, and logic), and the "strong" program in artificial intelligence (the mind as a computer). As distinguished neurologist Antonio Damasio put it in the 1990s, there had been a

> noticeable absence of a notion of *organism* in cognitive science and neuroscience . . . The notion of an integrated organism—the idea of an ensemble made up of a body proper and a nervous system . . . had little impact in shaping the standard conceptions of mind and brain.[3]

In the years since Damasio made this statement, scholars have begun to address this absence. New tools, such as functional magnetic resonance imaging (fMRI), allow us to study the workings of the brain in real time, and to explore its intimate and essential connection to the body. Research in genomics also calls attention to the biological dimension of who we are, and environmental concerns lead us to focus on living organisms and the ways in which human life can be threatened by human thought and behavior. Slowly, we are relinquishing our grip on a Cartesian worldview and searching for an alternative, embodied view of who we are.

Even before recent scholarship began to marshal considerable evidence against the mind/body split, Cartesian-style dualism had its critics. One of the most notable was psychologist, philosopher, and educator John Dewey, a leading public intellectual in the first half of the 20th century. Like his fellow "pragmatists" William James and Charles Sanders Peirce, Dewey rejected the idea that mind and body are distinct, as well as the method of radical doubt that had led the skeptics to embrace the idea of a chasm between the two. Indeed, the mind/body split was just one example of the dichotomous thinking, or "Either-Or philosophies" as he put it,[4] to which Dewey and his circle objected.

Dewey referred to his anti-dualist position as "the principle of continuity." Where some saw ruptures, he saw a progression—sometimes slower, sometimes more abrupt—as the individual grew and developed. The mind, and reason, were not fundamentally different from the body; instead mind was, as today's systems theorists would say, an "emergent" condition of the body—a newer, more complex property of a system that arises from the growth of smaller, less complex parts. "Continuity," Dewey wrote, "means that rational operations grow out of organic activities, without being identical with that from which they emerge."[5] It is far more plausible, and accords better with our everyday knowledge of the world, to think of rationality as something that develops gradually, both in our species over the millennia and in the individual progression from infant to adult, than to imagine that some unprecedented and radically different thing called mind appeared suddenly on the scene. Where would it come from? For the armchair Cartesian, this is no problem: a thinker can call up a category and build a world around it. But for a practical observer of the natural world, a pragmatist let's say, or a biologist, it's not so easy. There is a world out there to be explained, and explaining a *deus ex machina* appearance of mind runs contrary to science and common sense. As Charles Sanders Peirce trenchantly put it, "Let us not pretend to doubt in philosophy what we do not doubt in our hearts."[6]

At the same time, the mind/body dichotomy has a tenacious hold on the way we see the world. It is reified in our language—the terms "body" and "mind" are in heavy use in a variety of contexts—whereas a term emphasizing the unity of body and mind is sufficiently hard to find that Dewey resorted to speaking of the "body-mind" to make his point about continuity. "For a nondualist, this very 'mind-body problem' is a mistake because it presupposes that there are two distinct entities—body and mind—that must get yoked together," says Mark Johnson.[7]

Although Dewey's thinking has been influential in the education of children over the past century (his work inspired the "progressive education" movement, and he is still widely cited and discussed today in education circles), when I look around at what we do in universities in the US, I don't see much evidence of the principle of continuity. We still behave as if the cultivation of "the life of the mind" is our goal, and we attend to the student "body" primarily by offering athletics programs. Physical activity is essential to student well-being, but athletic and wellness programs are not integrated with academic programs—and sometimes participation on a sports team actually interferes with academic work. We generally don't design our pedagogy, or our campus classrooms and infrastructure, as if the mind and body were inseparable.

Embodiment

Contemporary scholars who share Dewey's anti-dualist approach to cognition often speak of the mind as "embodied," indicating the deep, complex, and necessary interconnections between body and mind. While they may continue to use the words "mind" and "body," they stress that the two are not distinct in the way we may naïvely think them to be, and that because mind is an emergent phenomenon, there is no clear line that can meaningfully be drawn between the two entities. In his celebrated books *Descartes' Error* and *The Feeling of What Happens*, neurologist Antonio Damasio amasses formidable evidence, from experimental research and from his clinical practice, of the inseparability of body and mind, and the essential role of the body in constituting—not just supporting—the mind. It is worth quoting Damasio at length, in a passage taken from *Descartes' Error*:

> Surprising as it may sound, the mind exists in and for an integrated organism; our minds would not be the way they are if it were not for the interplay of body and brain during evolution, during individual development, and at the current moment. The mind has to be first about the body, or it could not have been. On the basis of the ground reference that the body continuously provides, the mind can then be about many other things, real and imaginary.
>
> This idea is anchored in the following statements: (1) The human brain and the rest of the body constitute an indissociable organism, integrated by means of mutually interactive biochemical and neural regulatory circuits (including endocrine, immune, and autonomic neural components); (2) The organism interacts with the environment as an ensemble: the interaction is neither of the body alone or of the brain alone; (3) The physiological operations we call mind are derived from the structural and functional ensemble rather than from the brain alone: mental phenomena can be fully understood only in the context of an organism's interacting in an environment.[8]

Perhaps it is our resistance to thinking of ourselves as organisms—that is, as animals—that causes us to resist a more fully integrated view of mind and body. As a species we have worked hard to distinguish ourselves from other creatures; acknowledging the integrated organism that is our embodied selves feels threatening and unfamiliar in the face of habits of mind and culture that have been with us for centuries. But researchers and scholars are increasingly coming to see the many and fundamental ways in which what we call body and mind are inseparable, and the harm we do ourselves by denying this.

Long before Damasio wrote these words, the eminent psychologist of art Rudolf Arnheim and his mentors, the Gestalt psychologists, also chafed against the separation, so well reinforced in our language, between mind and body. Arnheim was concerned with *perception* and *cognition*, and found that these two words also needed to be merged into a single concept. When mind and body are thought of as radically separate, perception becomes a function of the body, which is then thought of in a mechanical way as using the senses to receive inputs from the environment. This naïve view holds that the eyes, ears, hands, mouth, and skin are collectors of data from the environment, and that these sensory organs forward their data directly to the brain for processing. Yet when one examines the neurological evidence, it is clear that the senses, far from being passive collectors, are an active part of a closely coupled interaction between person and environment.

In his classic book, *Visual Thinking*,[9] Arnheim's discussion of visual perception makes a compelling case for the active participation of the eye and the body in cognition. For example, eye movements help to select a target of vision, and these movements are "somewhere between automatism and willful response." Selecting a target of vision is crucial to cognition and is, in a sense, a problem-solving activity in that it involves "a restructuring of a given problem situation." Many bodily activities, such as movements of the head and torso, affect what we perceive, and precede conscious processing by the brain. Indeed the processing of visual signals (and a primitive form of abstraction) begins with the photochemistry of the eye, which allows us to perceive colors not as they are in the world, so to speak, but as a combination of primary colors for which our eyes have receptors. Our view of the world we live in is already shaped by the frequencies of light which our eyes have evolved to perceive.

Perception, argues Arnheim, is thus a very active part of cognition, not a function separate from it. If we see a distant car as larger than a nearby letterbox, he says, it is because "the perceptual situation itself contains aspects that assign to the image of the car a relative size different from the one it has in the retinal projection. . . . The cognitive feat is accomplished within perception itself."[10] Rather than embracing a model in which all information is sent entirely unprocessed to the brain, and having the brain correct erroneous impressions that the letterbox is gigantic because the retinal image is larger than that of the car, some processing happens at earlier stages, as part of the normal activity of the body-brain system.

Because of the deep, complex, and fundamental connection between perception and cognition, Arnheim feels it necessary to adopt an admittedly non-standard use of the word *cognition*, extending it to include "sensory perception, memory, thinking, learning."[11] He categorically rejects the notion that there is a separation, in perception, between information gathering and information processing, and opens his book with the assertion that "the collaboration of perceiving and thinking in cognition would be incomprehensible if such a division existed."[12] Further, Arnheim adds, "In order to interpret the functioning of the senses properly, one needs to keep in mind that they did not come about as instruments of cognition for cognition's sake, but evolved as biological aids for survival. From the beginning they aimed at, and concentrated on, those features of the surroundings that made the difference between the enhancement and the impediment of life. This means that perception is purposive and selective."[13] Damasio concurs: "To perceive an object, visually or otherwise, the organism requires both specialized sensory signals *and* signals from the adjustment of the body, which are necessary for perception to occur."[14]

Seen in this light, a mind/body integration appears much more plausible—and indeed necessary—than the schism we have come to take for granted. Perhaps if humans had evolved first and foremost to serve "cognition for cognition's sake" such a split would be more believable, and the brain in the vat might be worthy of discussion. Much as it may disappoint some of my colleagues in the academy, our greatest intellectual feats are not by themselves the purpose of evolution (if evolution can be said to have a purpose) but a byproduct of the capabilities we have developed as we sought to survive, reproduce, and flourish. The mind/body split is an ex-post-facto construction, not a biological truth. The central truth of our organismic selves is that our bodies are inseparable parts of our cognitive apparatus. Our learning environments should take this into account.

One of the ways I have entertained myself over the years I've spent thinking about these issues is by asking colleagues and academic acquaintances, "Where do you do your best thinking?" Infrequently I get the answer "at my desk" or "when I'm at my computer," but the overwhelming majority of the responses are something like, "when I'm in the shower." This answer comes in many flavors—when I'm running, working out, waking up, falling asleep, doing errands, knitting, and many more—but what they have in common is being in one's body, and perhaps engaging the unconscious and the emotions, to a greater extent than we might at a desk, focused consciously on the problem at hand. The humor of a cartoon like the one in Figure 2.1 comes in part from the flash of recognition we may feel.

If cognition is embodied, why is this not obvious to us? After all, it is we who are doing the thinking. Wouldn't we know? Most of the time, we are not aware of the contribution that our bodies make to cognition, just as we are not aware of our hearts beating or our viscera extracting nutrients from food. Cognitive psychologists talk about "cognitive load,"

Figure 2.1 I get some of my best ideas in the shower. How about you?

which is the amount of information we have to keep in mind at one time in order to perform a task. Too high a cognitive load is overwhelming; being able to "offload cognition" by keeping a notebook, by delegating to a subordinate, or by making an action so habitual that we don't have to give it much thought, frees us up to attend to other things. Damasio puts it well:

> As vision, hearing, and touch evolved, the attention usually allocated to their component of overall perception increased accordingly; thus the perception of the body proper more often than not was left precisely where it did, and does, the best job: *in the background.*[15]

For sound cognitive and evolutionary reasons, our bodies, as Mark Johnson says, "hide out" in cognition, seeming to confirm the false impression that our bodies are bystanders to the act of thinking.[16]

As I began to realize the importance of attending to the body in the classroom, I began questioning many of the assumptions I held. Among the first had to do with the language we use in higher education. We speak a lot about "active" learning, but we are usually referring to mental, not physical, action. We want students to grapple with problems, to question, to think through what a term or a concept means, rather than to see themselves as passive receptacles into which the professor pours her wisdom. But these activities rarely entail physical action beyond writing in a notebook or on a worksheet, or using a handheld clicker to respond to prompts in a large lecture. What if I ask students to stand and to move, to use their hands and bodies in a new way, as I did with my Lego exercise? What would be the effect on my students and their learning? On me? What would I have to do differently to introduce embodied thinking into my classroom? And how would the room itself need to change?

One of my inspirations as I explored these questions were the Kinesthetic Learning Activities (KLAs) being tried by faculty in other disciplines. I attended a workshop at a conference on computer science education where the leaders demonstrated KLAs that had us moving around the room to mimic sorting algorithms and other basic computing concepts. We were sorted by height, by age, and by other less conspicuous criteria. I'm not a computer scientist, but I came out of this workshop feeling that I had a better understanding of algorithms, and I certainly had gained an understanding of the value of activities that engage gross motor functions in the classroom.

The mind/body distinction has a firm hold on our culture, particularly in our colleges and universities. One of the most cherished values of the academy is "the life of the mind," by which scholars mean the free and unfettered play of reason. Although no one in the academy thinks it necessary to say so, this is a disembodied reason, with the body in a subordinate role as a convenient life support system for the brain. Only when we recognize that ***the life of the mind is the life of the body*** will we begin to radically remake our pedagogy and our learning spaces.

Interaction and Inquiry

Our Cartesian view of the world has not only concealed from us the role of the body in reason, but also the centrality of *lived human experience* as the source of knowledge. Contemporary intellectual life often centers around concepts that are regarded as timeless. In our academic search for transcendent truth, we have embraced a view of the world and of ourselves that exists out of time—and therefore out of the lived, biological, time-bound body. As a result, we have learned to conceal from ourselves how human thought and learning really happen.

How can we explain human reason and consciousness? Descartes' strategy was to *begin* with reason and derive from it all else, but that strategy only works in the abstracted, timeless, concepts-as-objects world of Enlightenment thought. If we take a biological, time-bound, evolutionary perspective, Descartes' approach won't wash.

Damasio's research offers strong confirmation of the insights of the pragmatists more than half a century earlier. Agreeing with Arnheim, Damasio asserts that there is no such thing as passive perception of the world; perception grows from interaction with one's surroundings.

> The organism continuously *acts* on the environment (actions and exploration did come first), so that it can propitiate the interactions necessary for survival. . . . Perceiving is as much about acting on the environment as it is about receiving signals from it.[17]

From an evolutionary point of view, this close coupling between organism and environment far precedes the development of consciousness, and if Damasio and others are correct, is a prerequisite for consciousness and for reason.

Mark Johnson describes his perspective, shared by Damasio, Merleau-Ponty, Dewey, and others, as "interactionist"—putting interaction at the core. For interactionists, mind and reason grow out of the body's (and of course the mind's) situated communication with its surroundings. To this Johnson contrasts the "objectivist" view, predominant in 20th-century Western philosophy, that denies—or is unconcerned with—how concepts might originate in embodied human activity. Objectivists, like William James' Greeks, are concerned with timeless universals and the logical relationship between them. An objectivist approach can, and has, generated capacious scholarly activity. To interactionists, however, this approach misses the point. Johnson says it cleverly:

> Objectivists about logic might protest, once again, that they are not concerned with the emergence of logic in modes of inquiry; rather, they will insist, their only interest lies in the internal structure of a self-enclosed logical system. To this I answer that the objectivist is entitled to the puzzle-solving and exploratory exercises of formal logic. It is

> always possible to run the system "off-line," as it were, disengaged from the context of actual human inquiry.[18]

Disengagement from the context of actual human inquiry is not a luxury we can afford if we are concerned with how students learn and how to best encourage and enhance their learning. The compelling evidence for the role of the embodied mind, the emotions, and interaction with the environment in human learning prompts us to rethink how we teach and learn in college and elsewhere.

Interaction in Education

Dewey, as a leading 20th-century philosopher and educator, thought deeply and wrote extensively about learning and education. He is considered the father of the "progressive school" movement of the first half of the 20th century, although he was also a (sympathetic) critic of many of the manifestations of progressive education. Dewey stressed the role of experience—several of his books have the word "experience" in their title—and of experience-based, active exploration, or *inquiry*, as the main driver of learning. Interaction between a person and her environment is a conversation between a person's interior states and the external circumstances in which she finds herself:

> The word interaction . . . assigns equal rights to both factors in experience—objective [i.e. external] and internal conditions. Any normal experience is an interplay of these two sets of conditions. Taken together, or in their interaction, they form what we call a *situation*. . . . The statement that individuals live in a world means, in the concrete, that they live in a series of situations. . . . It means . . . that interaction is going on between an individual and objects and other persons. . . . An experience is always what it is because of a transaction taking place between an individual and what, at the time, constitutes his environment.[19]

Furthermore, says Dewey, "Every genuine experience has an active side which changes in some degree the objective conditions under which experiences are had."[20] Learning is in its essence a dynamic process, taking place in a situation, over time.

In *Experience and Education*, a concise statement of Dewey's views published in 1938, more than 20 years after his first major work on education, Dewey contrasts traditional educational approaches with progressive approaches, noting both the failings of the traditional approaches and the ways in which some progressive schools misunderstood the nature of these failings and in so doing created new problems for students and teachers. In particular, Dewey criticized schools' tendencies to misunderstand the nature of experience:

> It is a great mistake to suppose . . . that the traditional schoolroom was not a place in which pupils had experiences. . . . [Instead,] the experiences which were had, by pupils and teachers alike, were largely of a wrong kind. How many students, for example, were rendered callous to ideas, and how many lost the impetus to learn because of the way in which learning was experienced by them? How many acquired special skills by means of automatic drill so that their power of judgment and capacity to act intelligently in new situations was limited? How many came to associate the learning process with ennui and boredom?[21]

Because Dewey believed that human learning is situated learning, all aspects of the schooling experience are significant. Students learn dispositions along with facts, aversions along with the alphabet, and develop either a taste or a distaste for learning.

In the 21st century, "experiential learning" has become something of a buzzword in higher education, and at many schools, including my own, experiential learning refers only to off-campus learning experiences—field trips, internships, service learning projects, and the like. These off-campus experiences can be enormously valuable, but by focusing on promoting them, we conceal the fact that *all* learning is experiential. Higher education should be creating a continuum of experiences for students, starting with rich, conducive, *on* campus learning environments that then connect to educative situations off campus.

When I first read Dewey's question about how many students had experiences that robbed them of their impetus to learn, I thought about my own experience in math classes throughout my long career in school. I recall weeping over my fourth-grade math homework; I can still see in my mind's eye the drawings of pumpkins arrayed around that multiplication table, so it must have been in the fall. Most of my math education did not drive me to tears, but the rote-learning and single-answer problems I was confronted with certainly gave me no pleasure or desire to continue beyond the math

I was required to take. I think that I might have been more positively disposed toward math today if I had had less, rather than more, math education. Or perhaps, as now believe, if I had been introduced to math concepts through craft projects such as the crocheted hyperbolic plane (see Interlude A). I did have experiences in those classrooms, but they were such that I was turned away from, rather than toward, mathematics.

In my classroom today, I work to teach to the situated, embodied learner; I think about what experiences they can have in my classroom that will build skills and knowledge, but also dispositions and a taste for the subject matter. One of my undergraduate courses, "Designing the Future World" (described in Interlude E), is an interdisciplinary course open to all majors, for which students can get social science general education credit. The class emphasizes "design thinking" as a problem-solving method particularly well suited to complex, open-ended problems. I give students a lot of hands on exercises, usually using clay, paper, Lego, Post-Its, pipe cleaners, or other craft materials. With prompts like "create a model of the place you would most like to study" or "make a poster that will educate others about how to overcome the challenges of recycling" or "show how you would change one feature of this building to accord with the principles of Universal Design," students spend between fifteen minutes and an hour working alone or with others to create an artifact, then explaining it to the rest of the class. For some exercises, students may spend some of their time searching the Internet for useful facts, but in my teaching I tend to place more emphasis on the ability to frame a problem, select an approach, and sketch a solution. As students work, they are active, engaged, talking, moving materials around as they explore possible solutions. I walk around the room as they work, briefly observing and listening, and paying particular attention to groups that are less engaged—quiet rather than conversing, sitting back rather than leaning in, with puzzled or blank expressions on their faces. These are the groups I visit first, and ask if they understand the instructions, or whether they are feeling stuck; a brief exchange is usually all it takes to get the group underway.

Even Descartes understood the value of wider experience compared to an exclusive diet of book learning. In his *Discourse on the Method* he recounts:

> As soon as my age permitted me to pass from under the control of my instructors, I entirely abandoned the study of letters, and resolved no longer to seek any other science than the knowledge of myself, or of the great book of the world. I spent the remainder of my youth in traveling, in visiting courts and armies, in holding intercourse with

> men of different dispositions and ranks, in collecting varied experience, in proving myself in the different situations into which fortune threw me, and, above all, in making such reflection on the matter of my experience as to secure my improvement. For it occurred to me that I should find much more truth in the reasonings of each individual with reference to the affairs in which he is personally interested, and the issue of which must presently punish him if he has judged amiss, than in those conducted by a man of letters in his study, regarding speculative matters that are of no practical moment, and followed by no consequences to himself, farther, perhaps, than that they foster his vanity the better the more remote they are from common sense; requiring, as they must in this case, the exercise of greater ingenuity and art to render them probable.[22]

What irony that this is the same man whose work, later in life, made him appear to students everywhere to be the very model of an armchair philosopher.

Notes

1. Johnson, M. (2007). *The meaning of the body: Aesthetics of human understanding* (p. 2). Chicago, IL: The University of Chicago Press.
2. James, W. (1916). *Some problems of philosophy* (pp. 53–54). New York, NY: Longmans, Green, & Co. Retrieved from https://archive.org/stream/someproblemsphil00jameuoft#page/n5/mode/2up.
3. Damasio, A. (1999). *The feeling of what happens: Body and emotion in the making of consciousness* (p. 40). San Diego, CA: Harcourt.
4. Dewey, J. (1938/1997). *Experience and education* (p. 82). New York, NY: Touchstone.
5. Dewey, J. (1938/2008). *Logic: The theory of inquiry* (p. 26). Carbondale, IL: Southern Illinois University Press.
6. Peirce, C. S. (1868). Some consequences of four incapacities. *Journal of Speculative Philosophy, 2*, 140–157. p. 140.
7. Johnson, M. (2006, Summer). Mind incarnate: From Dewey to Damasio. *Daedalus*, 46–54. p. 48.
8. Damasio, A. (1994). *Descartes' error: Emotion, reason, and the human brain* (pp. xx–xxi). New York, NY: Penguin Books.
9. Arnheim, R. (1969). *Visual thinking*. Berkeley, CA: University of California Press.
10. Arnheim, R. (1969). *Visual thinking* (p. 15). Berkeley, CA: University of California Press.
11. Arnheim, R. (1969). *Visual thinking* (p. 13). Berkeley, CA: University of California Press.
12. Arnheim, R. (1969). *Visual thinking* (p. 1). Berkeley, CA: University of California Press.
13. Arnheim, R. (1969). *Visual thinking* (p. 19). Berkeley, CA: University of California Press.

14. Damasio, A. (1999). *The feeling of what happens: Body and emotion in the making of consciousness* (pp. 146–147). San Diego, CA: Harcourt.
15. Damasio, A. (1994). *Descartes' error: Emotion, reason, and the human brain* (p. 233). New York, NY: Penguin Books.
16. Johnson, M. (2007). *The meaning of the body: Aesthetics of human understanding* (p. 47). Chicago, IL: The University of Chicago Press.
17. Damasio, A. (1994). *Descartes' error: Emotion, reason, and the human brain* (p. 225). New York, NY: Penguin Books.
18. Johnson, M. (2007). *The meaning of the body: Aesthetics of human understanding* (p. 110). Chicago, IL: The University of Chicago Press.
19. Dewey, J. (1938/1997). *Experience and education* (pp. 42–43). New York, NY: Touchstone.
20. Dewey, J. (1938/1997). *Experience and education* (p. 39). New York, NY: Touchstone.
21. Dewey, J. (1938/1997). *Experience and education* (p. 27). New York, NY: Touchstone.
22. Descartes, R. (2008). *A discourse on the method [e-Book]*. Retrieved from www.gutenberg.org/files/59/59-h/59-h.htm. Part I.

Interlude B: Molecular Models

One college subject where physical materials are often used is chemistry, particularly the notoriously challenging subject of organic chemistry, the bane of many a pre-med student. Molecular models may be constructed before class and passed around for students to look at, model making may be a part of laboratory sections, students may purchase a small molecular modeling kit for their own use, or all three. There is a long tradition of building molecular models in chemistry and biochemistry, and despite the development of software tools for representing molecular structure, the use of physical models continues not only in college but also, in some cases, in scientific research.

August Wilhelm von Hofmann, a German chemist, is credited with making the first physical models of molecules starting around 1860. His model of methane looks odd to our modern eyes because the atoms, represented by balls, were all in the same plane, but it is otherwise recognizable. A century and a half later, we know a great deal more about the characteristics of compounds and have several types of physical models available to represent them. Just as there are different sorts of maps, emphasizing different features of the thing represented (highways, topography, tourist attractions), there are molecular models that sacrifice accuracy in some areas in order to better portray particular properties of compounds.

Perhaps the most common sort of molecular model is the "ball-and-stick" variety. Hoffman's model of methane was of this sort, and the kits sold to chemistry students generally are as well. In these models, the balls represent the atoms in the molecule, and the sticks represent the bonds that hold the atoms together. Ball-and-stick models can be custom made (elegant but labor intensive), constructed from the generic materials supplied

Figure B.1 A "ball and stick" molecular model of Vitamin B12.

in molecular modeling kits, or even made from children's craft or construction materials (think Tinkertoys and Zometool, or toothpicks and Styrofoam).

Other models, particularly useful for inorganic chemistry and crystallography, are composed of closely packed spheres. In a common sodium chloride example the spheres are all the same size, although in fact the cations and anions are of different radius. As with ball-and stick models, accuracy in every detail is impossible, which means the model maker must choose which features to represent.

Figure B.2 Linus Pauling often posed with molecular models.

With the recent advent of inexpensive 3D printers, models for classroom use can be printed using molecular modeling software to design the molecule, and a computer file downloaded to the printer to create the physical model.

Students are not the only ones who use and benefit from physical models of molecules. In fact, for the first century or so of molecular models, physical models were the only variety available. Linus Pauling, winner of the Nobel Prize in chemistry in 1954, was a particular devotee of physical models, and is often pictured with them.

Figure B.3 James Watson, left, and Francis Crick with their double helix model of DNA.

James Watson and Francis Crick, co-discoverers of the double-helix structure of DNA, famously built a large physical model as a way of working out the structure of DNA, as well as a way of convincing other scientists. Max Delbrück, a biophysicist who saw Watson and Crick's model, was convinced.

> The whole business was like a child's toy that you could buy at the dime store, all built in this wonderful way that you could explain in *Life* magazine so that really a five-year-old can understand what's going on. That there was so simple a trick behind it. . . . This was the greatest surprise for everyone.[1]

Ironically, physical model devotee Linus Pauling, who had suggested a triple helix structure for DNA, was competing with Watson and Crick, but had failed to look at the critical X-ray diffraction image taken by Rosalind Franklin, the other runner-up in the race to identify the structure of DNA.

Even after the advent of computer graphics software that can represent molecules, physical models still serve a purpose for scientists. Reflecting this usefulness, in 2006 The Scripps Research Institute launched a service that makes physical models for the research community. Scripps professor Art Olsen says,

> The feedback I get from researchers who have these models is that they're amazed by how much the models are used. . . . A physical object is persistent. It's there. In contrast to virtual representations, people contemplate physical objects longer and interact with each other around them more.[2]

While computer representations have been enormously helpful to working scientists, and have many capabilities that physical models do not, the reverse is also true. "Now people are so used to seeing images on the computer that building a physical model can present challenges," according to Olson. "The prospect of making a solid model forces people to think about their molecule's physicality. They are confronted with such basic questions as 'Will it hold together?'"[3]

Notes

1. Judson, H. F. (1979). *The eighth day of creation* (p. 60). New York, NY: Simon & Shuster.
2. Ono, M. (2006, March 13). New service offers molecular models a.k.a. thinking tools. *The Scripps Research Institute News & Views*, *6*(9). Retrieved from www.scripps.edu/newsandviews/e_20060313/models.html.
3. Ono, M. (2006, March 13). New service offers molecular models a.k.a. thinking tools. *The Scripps Research Institute News & Views*, *6*(9). Retrieved from www.scripps.edu/newsandviews/e_20060313/models.html.

Thinking With Things 3

What does it mean to think *with* a thing? Usually we speak of thinking *about* things—a phrasing that expresses the activity of the observer and the inertness of the object or idea that is the focus of contemplation. The thinker has all the agency, and all the power, in the relationship between thinker and thought-about. Isn't this how it should be? To speak otherwise would be to engage in magical thinking, to give life to something that clearly does not have a life of its own. This would be the antithesis of rational thought; certainly this kind of thinking has no place in the academy. Yet just as Chapter 2 showed us that reason is neither dispassionate nor disembodied, perhaps our way of thinking about things can be more engaged, more interactive, more mutual than we ordinarily take it to be, without going to the extreme of magical thinking or animism. How can we make sense of the idea of "thinking with things"? When we are trying to understand embodied and situated learning, the phrase can have an intuitive appeal. It captures something worth pursuing that "thinking about things" does not.

When I first encountered the phrase "thinking with things," it struck a deep chord that continues to resonate. The phrase originates with Claude Lévi-Strauss, the celebrated French anthropologist, who studied traditional societies in Brazil and elsewhere. In his writing on the practice of totemism, he argued that indigenous people who adopted an animal as their group symbol or emblem do so not for survival reasons but for "intellectual" reasons. The animals "are chosen not because they are 'good to eat' (*bonnes à manger*) but because they are 'good to think [with]' (*bonnes à penser*)."[1]

In his book *The Savage Mind*, Lévi-Strauss argues strongly against the prevailing view that, for example, the absence of certain generic terms in the language of particular groups demonstrates "the supposed ineptitude of 'primitive people' for abstract thought."[2] People in traditional societies are in fact eminently rational, he asserts, and the presence or absence of certain terms reflects their different purposes, not an intellectual deficit.

In "thinking with" animals, plants, and other features of their surroundings (including human and "abstract" things such as kinship), indigenous people are practicing what Lévi-Strauss calls a *science of the concrete.* He cites many cases in which groups have developed enormously detailed classification systems with which they structure their understanding of the natural world.

> The proliferation of concepts, as in the case of technical languages, goes with more constant attention to properties of the world, with an interest that is more alert to possible distinctions which can be introduced between them. This thirst for objective knowledge is one of the most neglected aspects of the thought of people we call "primitive" . . . the universe is an object of thought at least as much as it is a means of satisfying a need.[3]

A science of the concrete, which Lévi-Strauss contrasts with modern Western science, in fact shares many of the characteristics of modern science. It uses close observation of the natural world, it requires human intelligence, and it structures and classifies natural and human phenomena. These structures may seem entirely irrational through the lens of science as we know it in the developed world, but they come out of a rational system whose outcomes reflect a different culture and set of purposes:

> The real question is not whether the touch of a woodpecker's beak does in fact cure toothache. It is rather whether there is a point of view from which a woodpecker's beak and a man's tooth can be seen as "going together" (the use of this congruity for therapeutic purposes being only one of its possible uses), and whether some initial order can be introduced into the universe by means of these groupings. . . . As a recent theorist of taxonomy writes: "Scientists do tolerate uncertainty and frustration, because they must. The one thing that they do not and must not tolerate is disorder . . . the most basic postulate of science is that nature itself is orderly . . ." The thought we call primitive is founded on this demand for order. This is equally true of all thought.[4]

A science of the concrete is not a "timid and stuttering form of [modern] science." Instead it is complete and coherent in itself; the two systems are "parallel modes of acquiring knowledge."[5]

A central activity of the science of the concrete is what Lévi-Strauss calls *bricolage*. Because there is no exact translation of this term, it is preserved even in the English translation of the book. The closest approximation in English might be "tinkering," because the bricoleur uses the things that are at hand to express a new idea by constructing something meaningful. The product of the bricoleur's work may be (using modern categories) a sculpture, a machine, or a narrative, or any other outcome of the combination of opportunity and imagination. The bricoleur is one who engages in an extended interaction with the physical and cultural environment—one who, in the words of Bamberger and Schön, has a "reflective conversation with materials."[6] Levi-Strauss says of the bricoleur:

> Consider him at work and excited by his project. His first practical step is retrospective. He has to turn back to an already existent set made up of tools and materials, to consider or reconsider what it contains, and finally and above all, to engage in a sort of dialogue with it and, before choosing between them, to index the possible answers which the whole set can offer to his problem. He interrogates all the heterogeneous objects of which his treasury is composed to discover what each of them could 'signify' and so contribute to the definition of a set which has yet to materialize. . . . A particular cube of oak could be a wedge to make up for the inadequate length of a plank of pine or it could be a pedestal—which would allow the grain and polish of the old wood to show to advantage . . . [the bricoleur] by inclination or necessity always remains within [the constraints imposed by a particular state of civilization].[7]

Thinking *with* a thing, as the bricoleur does, is at its core an interaction. Like thinking *about* a thing, it is also reflective, but the reflection takes place in action[8] rather than as a contemplative activity conducted after the fact, as it were from an armchair. The bricoleur "interrogates" the tools and materials the situation affords, engages in "a sort of dialogue with" them, and then reconfigures them to create a new meaning. The materials talk back to the maker, telling him what they are and are not good for, what they "signify." The artist Ben Shahn captures this when he writes about making a painting.

> So one must say that painting is both creative and responsive. It is an intimately communicative affair between the painter and his painting, a conversation back and forth, the painting telling the painter even as it receives its shape and form.[9]

This is not to suggest that any of these authors believe that tools, materials, or paintings are alive in the biological sense; instead, this way of speaking about the human relationship with the objects and ideas in our environment points to the possibility of a deep interplay, a generative interaction, between the bricoleur and those things that are available in his or her environment. The interplay of human intentions and what Gibson calls the "affordances"[10] of the environment (the features which afford, or support, particular activities, such as lifting, bending, drinking, bouncing) can profitably be seen as a dialogue or conversation, in which the human maker acts upon the environment, then responds to the alteration caused by that action through observing the new situation and, perhaps, modifying their next move based on the new information perceived.

Social psychologist Sherry Turkle is fascinated by bricolage and by the intensity of the relationships people can have with objects. She has coined the term *evocative object* to capture the special blend of thought and feeling that accompany an intimate relationship with an object.

> We find it familiar to consider objects as useful or aesthetic, as necessities or vain indulgences. We are on less familiar ground when we consider objects as companions to our emotional lives or as provocations to thought. The notion of evocative objects brings together these two less familiar ideas, underscoring the inseparability of thought and feeling in our relationship to things. We think with the objects we love; we love the objects we think with.[11]

Anything can be a thing to think with, although some things are more provocative, or more productive, than others. The fertility of a thing to think with depends on many factors, including the purposes and state of development of the thinker, and the qualities and affordances of the thing. In the remainder of the chapter, I offer one extended example of a suite of things explicitly designed to shape the thought of their users, young children of the late 19th and early 20th centuries.

Froebel Materials: An Important Early Example

A carefully designed set of pedagogical things to think with were extraordinarily influential in the late 19th and early 20th centuries. They were the Kindergarten materials developed by Friedrich Froebel, a German educator and natural scientist born in 1782. A lackluster student with a limited education and a very checkered resume—including apprenticeship to a woodsman, several positions as a tutor, two years spent studying and teaching the system of education pioneered by Swiss educator Johann Heinrich Pestalozzi, and another two years working under the direction of an eminent crystallographer. After his favorite brother died in 1813, Froebel started a school, initially for the purpose of educating his nephews. By 1826, enrollment had grown to more than 60 pupils, but internal disputes led to a decline such that by 1829 only five students remained. After working during the 1830s to establish schools and provide teacher training in Switzerland, Froebel shifted focus to the education of children younger than formal school-age, establishing his first Kindergarten in 1840 near Bad Blankenburg, Germany.[12]

Froebel's educational philosophy, as well as his methods, owe much to his teacher Pestalozzi, who in turn was inspired by the work of French philosopher (and botanist and composer) Jean-Jacques Rousseau. Rousseau's *Emile*, published in 1762, laid out his approach to the education of children. It was to be centered around the child, focused on what he needed for his development, rather than on delivering lectures to children to prepare them for adult knowledge. Rousseau's belief that "God makes all things good; man meddles with them and they become evil"[13] applies to children as well. At first very controversial, although eventually influential and widely read, *Emile* was an opening salvo of the Romantic era:

> Man's primary natural goals are, therefore, to measure himself against his environment, to discover in every object he sees those sensible qualities which may concern himself, so his first study is a kind of experimental physics for his own preservation. He is turned away from this and sent to speculative studies before he has found his proper place in the world. . . . Since everything that comes into the human mind enters through the gates of sense, man's first reason is a reason of sense-experience. It is this that serves as a foundation for the reason of the intelligence; our first teachers in natural philosophy are our feet, hands, and eyes. To substitute books for them does not teach us to reason, it teaches us to use the reason of others rather than our own; it teaches us to believe much and know little.[14]

Inspired by *Emile*, Pestalozzi created a way of teaching, and eventually a school, that promoted children's development through nature study, movement, music, and other activities. Pestalozzi believe that a child's natural desire to explore and learn, which he referred to as "self-activity," would, in a conducive environment and under the guidance of sympathetic adults, lead to the constructive development of the mind and the self.

We remember Froebel today not as an acolyte of Pestalozzi's revolutionary approach to teaching children—although he certainly was that—but because of his insight that schooling could begin at a younger age, given suitable learning materials and careful planning of activities, than was the custom at that time. Froebel developed a system of manipulatives and activities designed to introduce children of about five years old to sensorimotor activities involving structured singing, dancing, and play with small wooden blocks in basic geometric shapes that could be arranged on grid-lined work surfaces. His system also included crocheted spheres for infants, and a variety of activities with craft materials such as paper and yarn, used in a prescribed but flexible way. The 20 or so "gifts," as he called them, and the "occupations" in which the children engaged, were at the heart of Froebel's approach, which he named "Kindergarten."

All activities were designed by the naturalist and crystallographer to lead children to develop, through playful exploration, insight and intuition about the unity of nature, science, art, and spirituality, and their shared basis in qualities such as pattern, symmetry, number, and rhythm.

> Simply put, Froebel perceived that since the shapes of crystals—combinations of triangles and tetrahedrons, squares and cubes—are the outcome of the same natural laws that result in the growth of children, people, and entire societies, handling and manipulating models of these forms correctly would reveal and illuminate the logic of creation.[15]

Although the goals were lofty, infused with Romantic-era philosophy, the means were very direct, with an elegant simplicity. "Like Pestalozzi, Froebel made *objective work*, or object teaching, central to his pedagogy, recognizing that the handling of material things aided children in the development of their creative faculties."[16]

The most durable and generally most remembered of the Kindergarten materials are the small wooden blocks, made of maple and carefully crafted to a uniform size in simple geometric forms. They are the precursor of today's "unit blocks" but smaller and optimized for concentrated work at a table. In a Froebel Kindergarten, children could arrange dozens of similar blocks in patterns, then rearrange them at will. Their natural beauty, their feel in the hand, their suitability for holding between child-sized thumb and forefinger, made them elegantly well suited for exploring pattern, shape, symmetry. Children could grasp—literally, and figuratively as well—connections and principles for which they as yet had no words, but which they could see take shape as they manipulated the Froebel materials. The blocks support inquiry, experimentation, manipulation, and the growth of the child's understanding. In today's terminology, we would say that the materials, the ways of using them, and the patient attention of the teacher "scaffold" the child's development; Froebel said, perhaps more poetically, "From objects to pictures, from pictures to symbols, from symbols to ideas, leads the ladder of knowledge."[17]

Froebel died in 1852, a mere twelve years after starting his first school for young children in Bad Blankenburg. Yet the seed he had planted was so robust, and the women to whom he had preached his method were so determined, that "the radical, and curiously metaphysical, Kindergarten system"[18] spread around the world in the second half of the 19th century. In the United States, the first Kindergartens were established by German immigrants. The first English language school was founded in Boston in 1860 by Elizabeth Peabody, a Transcendentalist, educator, and daughter of a fascinating Massachusetts family. Through her example and writings, as well as those of countless other supporters of early childhood education, by 1908 there were more than 400 associations in the US, representing many thousands of Kindergartens.

Figure 3.1 Blocks from the third, fourth, fifth, and sixth Froebel gifts.

With dramatic spread, however, came the dilution of the core principles and materials of the Froebel system. Acolytes developed their own materials and activities, or modified existing ones, and by World War I, Kindergartens still bore the name but most lacked the careful and systematic approach to learning, and to learning materials, that the Froebel system represented.[19]

Froebel Kindergarten and Modern Art

The book *Inventing Kindergarten* by Norman Brosterman begins with a history of Froebel's philosophy, his methods, and, most particularly, the materials and practices he developed to teach young children about shape, pattern, and motion. The revelation of Brosterman's book, however, is the compelling circumstantial case he makes for the influence of the Froebel Kindergarten materials on modern art and design in the 20th century. Beginning around 1900, a radically new sort of art took shape, and although it was influenced by many factors, Brosterman has marshaled strong visual and historical evidence for the contribution of Kindergarten, which educated many millions of young children during the half-century before World War I, to this new way of seeing and representing.

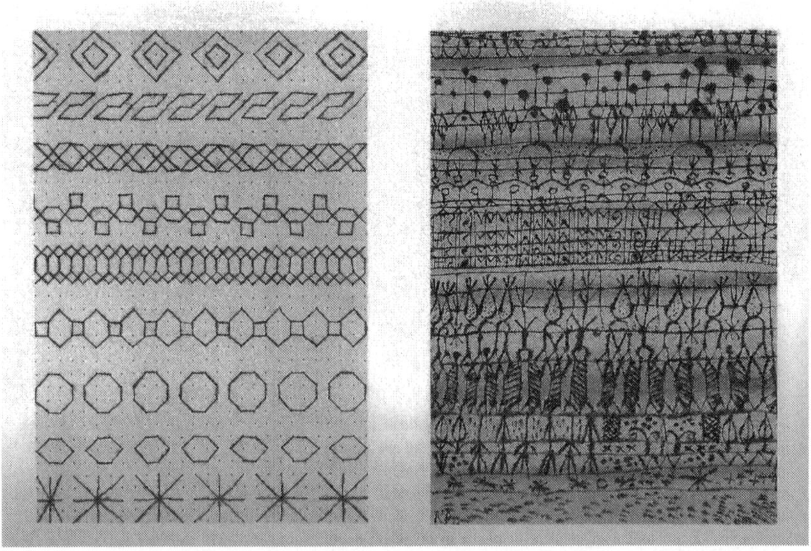

Figure 3.2 Kindergarten sewing on the left, Paul Klee painting on the right.

Piet Mondrian, Georges Braque, and architect Le Corbusier, along with the leaders of the Bauhaus—Walter Gropius, Josef Albers, Johannes Itten, Paul Klee, and Wassily Kandinsky—among many others, have been shown by Brosterman to have been taught using the Froebel materials, which were in very widespread use in Europe during the second half of the 19th century, when these giants of modernism were children. Would we have had Mondrian's grid paintings (see the resemblance to Figure 3.3), Braque's cubism, Le Corbusier's forms, and the streamlined, geometric aesthetic

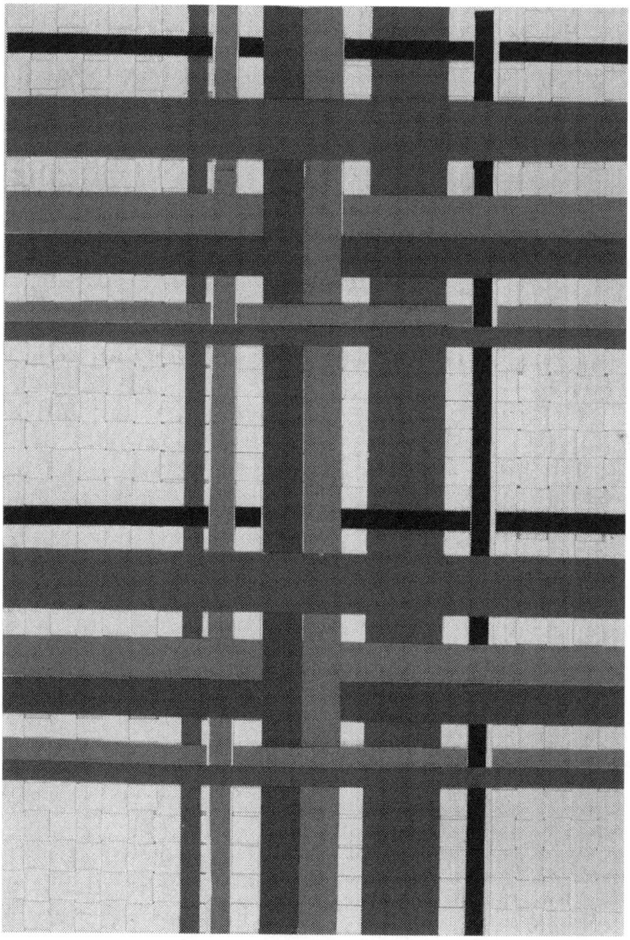

Figure 3.3 Kindergarten work from 1890, made with paper weaving, and resembling the work of Piet Mondrian.

of the Bauhaus without Froebel? Possibly, but Brosterman's argument is compelling.

In 1870, a decade after Elizabeth Peabody founded her Boston Kindergarten, Anna Wright moved her young family from Wisconsin to a Boston suburb. Six years later, as her son recalled decades afterward, she traveled to Philadelphia to visit the Centennial Exposition of 1876, which drew visitors from across the country to a celebration of American technology, economy, and culture. One of the exhibits was the small Kindergarten Cottage, where classes were held in full view of the visiting public. Anna Wright may already have known about Froebel Kindergarten, and indeed it is possible that she already had the Froebel materials in her home, but her visit to the Kindergarten exhibit seems to have reinforced her interest, since in her son Frank's reminiscences the Centennial Exposition was a turning point.

You may already have guessed that Anna's son was Frank Lloyd Wright, who grew up to be a titan of American architecture. Looking at Wright's rectilinear designs and his extensive use of nature and geometric forms, one cannot help but see the influence of the Froebel aesthetic (for one example, see Figure 3.4). Wright was in fact quite explicit about the impact on him of the Froebel materials, reminiscing fondly about them with statements like, "Eventually I was to construct designs in other mediums. But the smooth cardboard triangles and maple-wood blocks were most important.

Figure 3.4 Illustration, from an 1877 Kindergarten guide, of a house made from the blocks of Froebel's 6th gift.

All are in my fingers to this day" and "I soon became susceptible to constructive pattern *evolving in everything I saw*. I learned to 'see' this way and when I did, I did not care to draw casual incidentals of nature. I wanted to *design*."[20]

Froebel Kindergarten and Modern Science

Biographies of influential thinkers often do not discuss whether, or where, they went to Kindergarten, preferring to focus on later experiences. This reflects an implicit presumption that adolescent and adult experiences are the primary formers of adult work. An exception is sometimes made for childhood trauma as an influence on the mature professional, and biographers may delve into family dysfunction, but other effects of early experiences on cognition are seldom explored. Research on finger counting systems used to teach numeracy to children, however, shows that trace evidence of finger counting remains in adult performance on number manipulation tasks.[21] Similarly, it is entirely plausible that a system such at Froebel's could, consciously or not, affect the adult performance of Kindergartners. Brosterman has made a strong case for the impact on 20th century artists. Does the evidence permit us to make an analogous case for the most creative scientists of the same historical period?

That the Froebel approach should also influence scientists is not far-fetched. Froebel himself was a scientist and naturalist, and the materials he developed, in their geometric patterns and symmetries, show the stamp of the crystallographer's mind. Froebel had worked for a time under the direction of Professor Christian Samuel Weiss, who was the first to formulate an understanding of crystals based on their underlying, rather than surface, properties. Only a few years earlier, Dalton and Gay-Lussac had first applied atomic theory to chemistry, seeming to confirm the popular Platonic idea that there are "building blocks of nature." As Brosterman writes, "It was the genius of Froebel's mentor Weiss to recognize that the number, type, and relative *direction* of a specimen's observable geometric symmetries were a consequence of its unique internal structure and would ultimately reveal its specific chemical composition."[22] It is not a stretch to think that the Froebel materials would appeal to young children with a scientific or mathematical bent, or create in particular young children an inclination toward deep study of the ideas and patterns of nature. What do we know about Froebel Kindergarten and scientists of the 20th century?

Perhaps the most interesting case is that of physicist Richard Feynman, the brilliant, quirky Nobel laureate who was also famously a visual thinker. One of several lasting contributions he made to science is the Feynman diagram, a visual representation of an equation. In a 1966 talk to science teachers, Feynman recalls his early childhood education at the hands of his father:

> When my mother was carrying me, it is reported—I am not directly aware of the conversation—my father said that "if it's a boy, he'll be a scientist." How did he do it? He never told me I should be a scientist. He was not a scientist; he was a businessman, a sales manager of a uniform company, but he read about science and loved it.[23]

Feynman's father bought "a whole lot of rectangular floor tiles from someplace in Long Island City."[24] Father and son played with the tiles, and Mel taught his son to make patterns with the different colored tiles. In telling this story Feynman asserts that "mathematics is looking for patterns."[25] In a parenthetic note, Feynman continues,

> The fact is that this education had some effect. We had a direct experimental test at the time I got to kindergarten. We had weaving in those days. . . . We used to weave colored paper through vertical strips to make patterns. The kindergarten teacher was so amazed that she sent a special letter home to report that this child was very unusual, because he seemed to be able to figure out ahead of time what pattern he was going to get, and made amazingly intricate patterns. So the tile game did do something to me.[26]

Absent from Feynman's account is the fact that his mother, Lucille, trained as a Froebel Kindergarten teacher at Felix Adler's Ethical Culture School in New York, not long before her first child, Richard, was born.[27] No doubt Richard's father was a strong influence on him, but the young Richard not only would have practiced with his father's colored tiles, but likely would have spent much time with the paper weaving and other Kindergarten materials, which his mother would almost certainly have had at home. As a first-born child, a son, and one for whom his parents had such ambition, it is implausible that his mother would not use the knowledge she had gained at the Ethical Culture School to shape his development—indeed it is possible that she sought her training, as many mothers did, precisely in order to educate the children she hoped to have.

Was the remarkable, visual, unorthodox Feynman's way of seeing the world profoundly influenced by the Kindergarten system as he encountered

Figure 3.5 A page of examples of patterns that can be made with flat sticks, Froebel's eighth gift, from an 1859 Belgian manual.

it in his own home? It's hard to imagine that he was not significantly shaped by a way of thinking and doing that had attracted his mother, even before his birth. Because Feynman did not speak explicitly of any Kindergarten experience—unlike Wright and others—and in fact put it in eclipse when he told the story of what made him a scientist, we may never know, but the same circumstantial case can be made by considering the characteristics of the Froebel system, the formal resemblances between Froebel Kindergarten output and Feynman's diagrams, and the implausibility of thinking that Froebel the scientist would have influenced only artists and architects and not those scientists who had early immersion in the Kindergarten system.

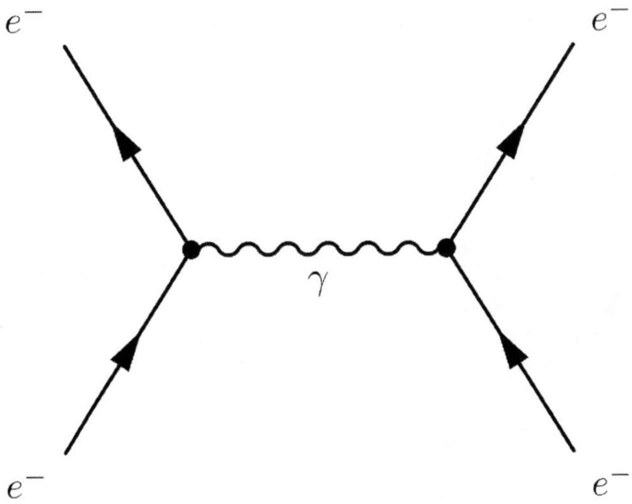

Figure 3.6 An example of a very simple Feynman diagram.

Another brilliant 20th century physicist, J. Robert Oppenheimer, best known for his work heading Los Alamos Laboratory during the World War II development of the atomic bomb, seems not to have attended Kindergarten, but was a student at the Ethical Culture school in New York starting at the age of 7.[28] The sheltered child of well-to-do parents, he was given books and materials that catered to any interest he showed. At age 5 he traveled to Germany to meet his father's family, where his uncle observed him playing with blocks and gave him a book on architecture, and a box of minerals, labeled with their Latin and German names. Inspired by this gift, collecting and studying minerals became a primary focus of Robert's childhood leisure activities. Another activity was continued play with blocks; later in life he described his three passions around ages 10 to 12 as "minerals, writing poems and reading, and building with blocks still—architecture"[29]

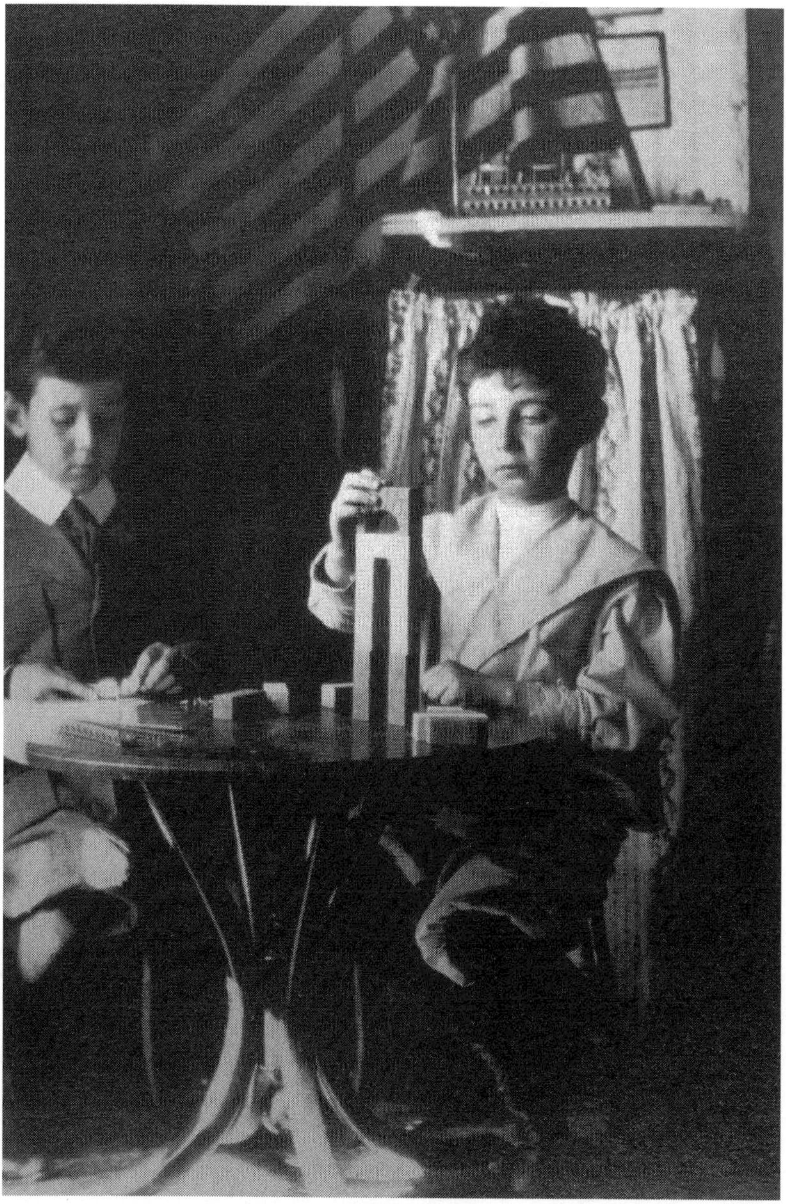

Figure 3.7 J. Robert Oppenheimer, right, around age 10, with his younger brother Frank.

His younger brother, Frank Oppenheimer, also attended the Ethical Culture school and also became a physicist, but when his career was thwarted by McCarthyism he turned to teaching, first at a high school and then at the university level. He developed a very object-oriented way of teaching physics at the college level, what he called a "Library of Experiments," and was the inspired founder of San Francisco's renowned Exploratorium, a uniquely hands-on science museum that supports sensory exploration of natural and physical phenomena. (More about the Exploratorium is to come in Chapter 5.)

The celebrated futurist and originator of "design science," Buckminster Fuller, was another product of Froebel Kindergarten, and his eclectic, category-defying mix of science, art, and engineering are perhaps the essence of the integration that Froebel sought to express with his system. Like Wright, the adult Fuller wrote of his early encounter with Kindergarten materials, and like Feynman, his work caused a stir among his teachers. Froebel's 19th gift was "peas work," a system for making three dimensional structures that consisted of partially cooked peas—or perhaps better, pea-sized spheres of soft clay—and sticks like toothpicks (Figure 3.8). A child was to build by anchoring the ends of the sticks in the peas, rather as a modern-day child would build with the construction playthings Tinkertoys or K'Nex, anchoring rods into connectors. Fuller recalled his encounter with the 19th gift:

> One of my first days at Kindergarten the teacher brought us some toothpicks and semi-dried peas, and told us to make structures. With my bad sight, I was used to seeing only bulks. I had no feeling at all about structural lines. The other children, who had good eyes, were familiar with houses and barns. Because I couldn't see, I naturally had recourse to my other senses. When the teacher told us to make structures, I tied to make something that would work. Pushing and then pulling, I found that the triangle held its shape when nothing else did. The other children made rectangular structures that seemed to stand up because the peas held them in shape. The teacher called all the other teachers in primary school to take a look at this triangular structure. I remember being surprised that they were surprised.[30]

Fuller is perhaps best known as the creator of the geodesic dome, which—like his novel Kindergarten construction—is based on triangles. The triangles of the geodesic dome are inscribed inside a spherical or semi-spherical shape (see Figure 3.9).

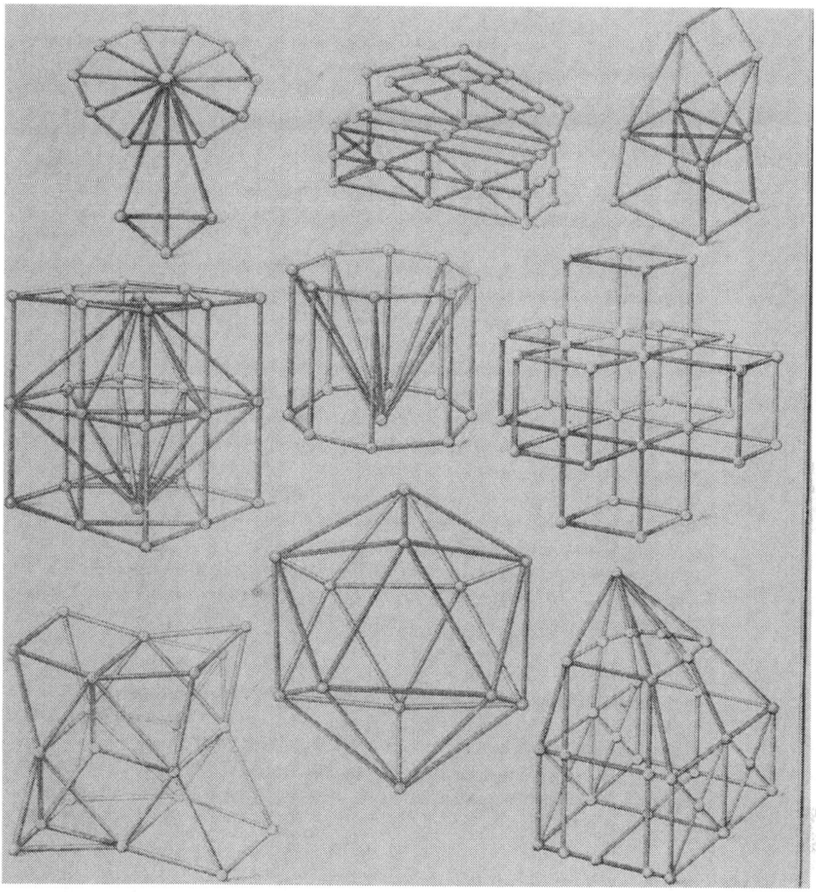

Figure 3.8 A page from an 1858 teachers' guide to the Froebel system, showing "peas work," the 19th gift.

Today there remain very few early childhood programs using Froebel's methods and materials. Yet his influence lives on, most conspicuously in the universal use of the term "Kindergarten" for the schooling of 5-year-olds, but also in the impact that his work had on his successors in early childhood education, including Maria Montessori and Rudolf Steiner (the inspiration behind Waldorf schools), as well as the originators of the Reggio Emilia system. All of these methods, although varied in approach and philosophy, emphasize extended exploration and use of physical materials, and study of patterns in nature and in mathematics. A "thinking with things" approach to early learning is one of the threads that travels as a through line from Pestalozzi

Figure 3.9 A geodesic dome designed by Buckminster Fuller at what is now the Montreal Biosphere museum.

to Froebel to Montessori, Waldorf, and Reggio. As most of today's Kindergartens become increasingly oriented to academic abstractions like reading, writing, and mathematics, instead of child-directed encounters with the physical world, what will be the impact on future artists, scientists, and others who are so critical to the development of our culture and our knowledge systems?

Notes

1. Lévi-Strauss, C. (1964). *Totemism* (R. Needham, Trans., p. 89). London, UK: Merlin Press.
2. Lévi-Strauss, C. (1966). *The savage mind*. Chicago, IL: The University of Chicago Press.

3. Lévi-Strauss, C. (1966). *The savage mind* (pp. 2–3). Chicago, IL: The University of Chicago Press.
4. Lévi-Strauss, C. (1966). *The savage mind* (p. 9). Chicago, IL: The University of Chicago Press.
5. Lévi-Strauss, C. (1966). *The savage mind* (p. 13). Chicago, IL: The University of Chicago Press.
6. Bamberger, J., & Schön, D. A. (1983). Learning as reflective conversation with materials: Notes from work in progress. *Art Education, 36*(2), 68–73.
7. Lévi-Strauss, C. (1966). *The savage mind* (pp. 18–19). Chicago, IL: The University of Chicago Press.
8. Schön, D. A. (1983). *The reflective practitioner: How professionals think in action.* New York, NY: Basic Books.
9. Shahn, B. (1957). *The shape of content* (p. 49). Cambridge, MA: Harvard University Press.
10. Gibson, J. J. (1977). The theory of affordances. In R. Shaw & J. Bransford (Eds.), *Perceiving, acting, and knowing: Toward an ecological psychology* (pp. 67–82). Hillsdale, NJ: Lawrence Erlbaum.
11. Turkle, S. (2007). *Evocative objects: Things we think with* (p. 5). Cambridge, MA: The MIT Press.
12. Wasmuth, H. (2020). *Fröbel's pedagogy of kindergarten and play: Modifications in Germany and the United States.* New York, NY: Routledge.
13. Rousseau, J.-J. (2004). *Emile [e-Book]* (B. Foxley, Trans., p. 4). Retrieved from www.gutenberg.org/files/5427/5427-h/5427-h.htm.
14. Rousseau, J.-J. (2004). *Emile [e-Book]* (B. Foxley, Trans., p. 103). Retrieved from www.gutenberg.org/files/5427/5427-h/5427-h.htm.
15. Brosterman, N. (1997). *Inventing kindergarten* (p. 25). New York, NY: Harry N. Abrams.
16. Brosterman, N. (1997). *Inventing kindergarten* (p. 34). New York, NY: Harry N. Abrams.
17. Quoted in Barnard, H. (Ed.). (1884). *Papers on Froebel's kindergarten: With suggestions on principles and methods of child culture in different countries* (p. 178). Syracuse, NY: C. W. Bardeen.
18. Brosterman, N. (1997). *Inventing kindergarten* (p. 13). New York, NY: Harry N. Abrams.
19. Brosterman, N. (1997). *Inventing kindergarten.* New York, NY: Harry N. Abrams.
20. Quoted in Brosterman, N. (1997). *Inventing kindergarten* (pp. 138–139). New York, NY: Harry N. Abrams.
21. Domahs, F., Moeller, K., Huber, S., Willmes, K., & Nuerk, H. (2010). Embodied numerosity: Implicit hand-based representations influence symbolic number processing across cultures. *Cognition, 116*, 251–266.
22. Brosterman, N. (1997). *Inventing kindergarten* (p. 24). New York, NY: Harry N. Abrams.
23. Feynman, R. (1999). *The pleasure of finding things out* (p. 174). New York, NY: Basic Books.
24. Feynman, R. (1999). *The pleasure of finding things out* (p. 174). New York, NY: Basic Books.
25. Feynman, R. (1999). *The pleasure of finding things out* (p. 175). New York, NY: Basic Books.
26. Feynman, R. (1999). *The pleasure of finding things out* (p. 175). New York, NY: Basic Books.
27. Gleick, J. (1992). *Genius: The life and science of Richard Feynman.* New York, NY: Pantheon.

28. Monk, R. (2012). *Robert Oppenheimer: A life inside the center.* New York, NY: Doubleday.
29. Smith, A. K., & Weiner, C. (Eds.). (1980). *Robert Oppenheimer: Letters and recollections* (p. 3). Stanford, CA: Stanford University Press.
30. Quoted in Brosterman, N. (1997). *Inventing kindergarten* (p. 84). New York, NY: Harry N. Abrams.

Interlude C: Diagrams

A diagram—a graphic representation of a thing, a system, or a phenomenon—is a terrific thing to think with. These graphic representations take a wide variety of forms, and occur across the disciplines. They help to capture existing knowledge, provoke questions that may lead to new knowledge, and support and structure the learning of students.

Maps

To illustrate how a graphic representation can perform all these functions, let's start with an everyday example: the map. Typically, a map is a two-dimensional depiction of a geographic area, constituting a sort of model of a particular terrain. There are many variations, of course, but since we are focusing on the everyday, let's stick with two-dimensional images, on paper or (these days) online.

Road maps are the most common type in everyday use. On paper or in digital form on GPS systems, road maps help travelers find their way from a point of origin to a destination. The canonical paper road map emphasizes streets, intersections, highways, interchanges, political boundaries and names (cities, states), and may include major landmarks. Map scale and types of roads, for example, are often indicated in a key supplied with the map. These maps capture and communicate a wealth of existing knowledge that help motorists to find their way, whether they are seeking the fastest and most efficient route or a leisurely trip on back roads. Users do not need to be familiar with a particular region in order to use these maps successfully, making basic knowledge about the layout of a geographic area accessible to a broad public.

Maps can also stimulate questions leading to new knowledge. For the tourist, a map may invite questions about a new city, a state park or wilderness area, or a region laced with particularly curvy roads. The truck driver may wonder about the frequency of rest stops, the speed limit, the number of hills, and the availability of trucker turnouts for rest and safety. Even locals, who grew up experiencing their region through the windshield or on foot may discover a connection between known locations, or new routes to familiar places, by looking at their home terrain with a bird's-eye view. Specialty maps used by geologists, urban planners, watershed managers, oceanographers, and a vast number of other professionals can also provoke questions and invite investigation by those trained to read these maps intended for experts.

Finally, these maps support and structure learning. Novices learn to associate features of a map with features of a territory. Typical road maps highlight such conventions as putting the compass point North at the top of the map, emphasizing roads while ignoring elevation, highlighting cities and towns but not watershed boundaries or the presence of trees, portraying distance but not climate, and so forth. Road maps tell the user what is worthy of attention and what is not. They support the motorist but not the hiker, thereby reinforcing 20th-century "car culture" and an urban or suburban bias.

At the same time, maps are a wonderful teaching tool. Because they come in many forms, teachers can ask students to compare, for example, a road map with a topographic map. With this simple exercise students can learn that maps are not perfect depictions of territories. They are created with assumptions about who will be using them and what the users will be interested in knowing. No map is "accurate" or "perfect." In fact, maps derive their usefulness from their incompleteness, the fact that they leave out some things while highlighting others. Imagine trying to drive from Atlanta to Seattle on back roads using satellite photos: you would have to discern where roads were even when they were covered by trees or camouflaged by terrain. You might not be able to distinguish an intersection from an overpass. You would labor to pick out the features salient to your trip from the unimportant details. It's the useful omissions and distortions in maps that give them value. The map is not the territory . . . and it shouldn't be.

In his classic book, *How to Lie with Maps*, Mark Monmonier begins, "Not only is it easy to lie with maps, it's essential. . . . To avoid hiding critical information in a fog of detail, the map must offer a selective, incomplete view of reality."[1] The "little white lies" that make maps useful, however, can also be exploited by the biased and the unscrupulous, and it is important for students to learn to distinguish between the relatively benign and the insidious. What does the map highlight? What does it obscure? Whose interests might it serve to portray an area in this way? Who gets the spotlight and who or what is left in the shadows? The racist mid-20th-century practice of "redlining" drew a line (sometimes literally) around minority neighborhoods, designating them as a risky place for mortgage lending and thereby depriving borrowers, regardless of their income, access to federally guaranteed home loans. Maps that show which sites have significant levels of pollution would alert residents to the dangers they faced, but such maps are not readily available to communities. If the most common maps displayed risks (drought, flooding, pollution, heat islands, and more) instead of just roads, and students learned to read and understand these, how might civic life be different?

The Periodic Table

The same principles and questions can be applied to discipline-specific representations and diagrams, from the most common to the most esoteric. For a familiar example, consider the periodic table of the elements.

This staple of science education is so immediately familiar in its overall appearance that it has sparked many humorous imitations—the periodic table of vegetables, of wine, of sandwiches, of emotions, and so on. For students who learn how to use the Periodic Table, it helps them to remember many of the features of chemical elements, and grouping them into color-coded families imparts further information about their characteristics. Furthermore, by organizing the elements into rows, columns, and colored groups, an otherwise-overwhelming complexity is reduced. (As we will see in Chapter 4, this chunking and categorization are aids to memory.)

As with a map, the Periodic Table also presents an opportunity to ask what is not represented. Russian chemist Dmitrii Mendeleev first described the Periodic Law and its associated table in 1869, noting that the properties of the elements repeat themselves with increasing atomic weights. Two years later, based on the gaps in the table he had created, Mendeleev predicted the discovery of ten new elements. In the ensuing century and a half, many more have been discovered, partly on the basis of gaps and absences in the table. Because of this, the Periodic Table has evolved over time, now showing far more elements, and elements of different kinds (the rare earth and transuranium elements, for example). The Periodic Table has provoked inquiry, and as research yielded results, the tool itself has evolved.[2]

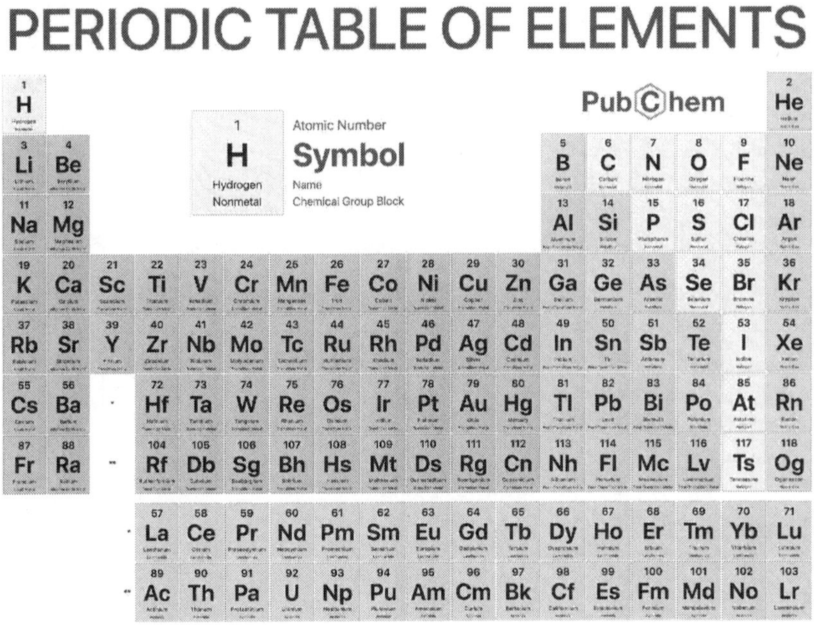

Figure C.1 A typical representation of the periodic table of elements.

Although the Periodic Table shown in Figure C.1 is more or less the one every schoolchild is taught, there have been a proliferation of representations of the Periodic Table since Mendeleev's first attempt. Mazurs[3] surveyed the cacophony of representations and, by grouping those that are essentially similar, came up with 146 different types. Many, like Mendeleev's original, are in tabular form, but many others use spirals, concentric circles, or figure-eight type curves on which the various elements are arrayed. Writing in 1974, Mazurs deemed the helical structure shown in Figure C.2 to be "the best table for presenting the Periodic Law in all its details."[4]

Rudolf Arnheim advocated strongly for the use of multiple representations. "The usual illustrations in textbooks . . . help to make a problem visible, but they also freeze it . . . they tempt the student to mistake accidental circumstances for essential ones."[5] Showing students a variety of representations of the elements is a great way to prompt inquiry. What does one representation emphasize that others do not? Which representations are most useful and for what purposes? Did you learn something from an unusual representation that you didn't learn from the standard tabular form of the Periodic Table? Are there omissions in any of the representations, and

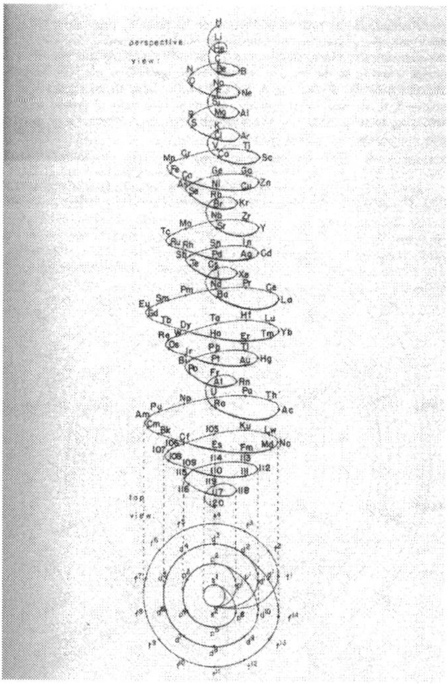

Figure C.2 A periodic table in the form of a helix, first created by George Schaltenbrand in 1920.

do they all omit the same things? Modeling phenomena with diagrams is important for students to learn as it is essential to the practice of science. It has the added advantage of making student thinking visible both to instructors and to fellow learners.[6] With a variety of mental models at their disposal, students may become more flexible in their thinking about chemical phenomena, and may also come to see that any particular representation is not fixed for all time and can be challenged.

It is not unusual for graphic representations to evolve as scientific knowledge evolves and changes. While some representations are abandoned, others, like the Periodic Table, change. Feynman diagrams, discussed in Chapter 3, are another interesting case. Physicist Richard Feynman developed the diagrams as an aide to calculations in quantum field theory. As quantum field theory began to be eclipsed by successor theories, one might think that the use of Feynman diagrams would fade away. Instead, they were adapted by the physics community for use with a host of other theories, well beyond their original application. Once physicists had learned to use the diagrams, they found other uses for them.[7]

Logic Models

As a professor of social science, I have also used diagrams and other graphic representations to good effect. I taught a grant writing course to masters students who were working with community-based nonprofit organizations. Chronically short of funds, these organizations were dependent on grants for a significant part of their budget, and the ability to write a compelling grant proposal was a much sought-after skill. A graphic tool called a "Logic Model" was coming into widespread use in the philanthropic community, and a request for funding that included a clear and well-thought-out logic model would be more compelling than one without.

Logic models can take many forms, but fundamentally they are a representation, usually in graphic form, of the cause-and-effect assumptions underlying a proposed social program. They are essentially a sequential if-then story about what the program designers believe will happen if they have the resources, and implement the activities, of the program they propose. (See Figure C.3 for a schematic.) One example I used in teaching was a program to prevent childhood lead poisoning. To design an effective program to prevent childhood lead poisoning, you need many things. What are the primary causes of childhood lead poisoning? Where are the case numbers the highest? Is this because this is where the best detection is done, or because children in this location are most at risk? What might the most effective interventions be? How will communities respond to these

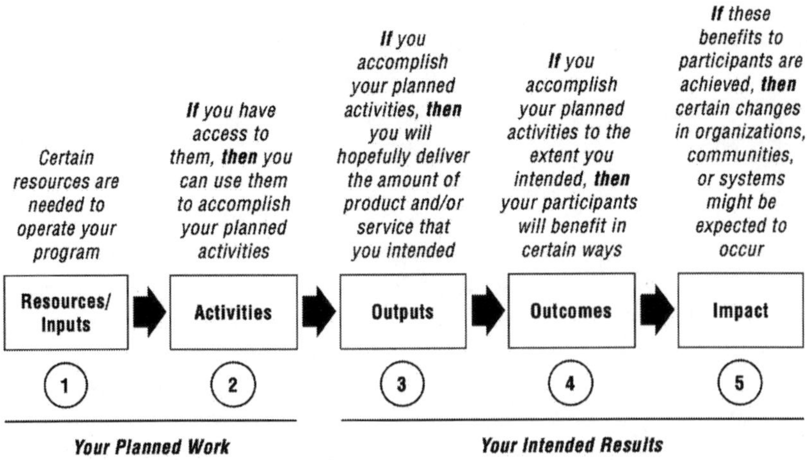

Figure C.3 Basic components of a logic model.

interventions? What organizations are most likely to join this campaign, and what motivates them?

The best logic models are supported by a clearly articulated theory of change (what will most effectively make positive change in this situation?) I found that my students were eager to jump in and propose activities that could be conducted ("make a brochure on lead poisoning to distribute in schools!" and "do finger-stick blood tests at playgrounds!") without carefully thinking through the strengths and weaknesses of existing prevention programs, the resources available in the community, the attitudes of parents toward outside medical intervention, the chances of cooperation from landlords and day care centers, issues of medical privacy, and many other factors that should be considered in designing an effective program.

Teaching my students to use logic models forced them to slow down and look carefully at their goals, their assumptions, and what might go wrong with their plans. When they had to spell out the logic of their proposed program they would see the holes in their arguments and challenge their own assumptions. Even more powerfully, by creating a logic model in a standardized graphic form, they could share their work with classmates and with me. Working together, debating goals and assumptions, students' logic models always became more robust and better attuned to the setting they were addressing. Even greater improvements are made when program designers work closely with the communities affected by the programs. Logic models provide a fairly simple tool that can be using in a participatory design process in which all stakeholders have a voice in program design. Although logic models can be created on a whiteboard or distributed as a photocopied document, my experience is that the most effective conversations happen around a tabletop covered with a giant piece of paper—I try always to have a big roll of butcher paper in my classroom—which participants can draw on and annotate as the discussions about program design evolve. The paper becomes a record of the discussions and captures the thinking behind the design, and when anyone can participate in the creation of this design artifact, it sends a powerful message about shared authority and responsibility.

Notes

1. Monmonier, M. (1991). *How to lie with maps* (p. 1). Chicago, IL: The University of Chicago Press.
2. Mazurs, E. (1974). *Graphic representations of the periodic system during one hundred years* (2nd ed.). Tuscaloosa, AL: The University of Alabama Press.

3. Mazurs, E. (1974). *Graphic representations of the periodic system during one hundred years* (2nd ed.). Tuscaloosa, AL: The University of Alabama Press.
4. Mazurs, E. (1974). *Graphic representations of the periodic system during one hundred years* (2nd ed., p. 108). Tuscaloosa, AL: The University of Alabama Press.
5. Arnheim, R. (1969). *Visual thinking* (p. 182). Berkeley, CA: University of California Press.
6. Lehrer, R., & Schauble, L. (2010). What kind of explanation is a model? In M. K. Stein & L. Kucan (Eds.), *Instructional explanations in the disciplines* (pp. 9–22). Boston, MA: Springer.
7. Kaiser, D. (2009). *Drawing theories apart: The dispersion of Feynman diagrams in postwar physics*. Chicago, IL: The University of Chicago Press.

How Things Shape Our Thinking 4

The Kindergarten materials discussed in Chapter 3 are an exemplar of how a system of things can influence the habits of mind and the visual culture of adults, long after they have left school. This chapter builds on that insight, asking about some of the many ways in which things influence adult cognition. As embodied thinkers and learners interact with their environment, how do things—especially things within reach—support and shape thinking?

Individual Thinking

In this section, I discuss a number of ways in which our thinking as individuals is influenced, inspired, and constrained by the things with which we interact. In a later section of this chapter, the focus turns to social thinking and interaction.

Long-Term Memory

Perhaps the most commonly understood way that things help us think is that they support and prompt memory. From the souvenir and the heirloom to the string tied around the finger, the daily planner, the online calendar, and the smartphone alarm, the use of things as a memory aid is so ubiquitous as to hardly need comment. Still, some historical examples demonstrate to us how ancient and how deeply engrained the human reliance on physical memory aides is.

String or twine is arguably one of the most ancient human technologies, although because it consists simply of perishable twisted plant or animal fiber, the archaeological record is very limited. Still, there is good evidence of the reliance in preliterate cultures on knots made in string (or rope or leather thongs) to keep a calendar and record numbers, or to support memory and recall of cultural traditions and narratives.[1] From around the world come accounts of groups using strings of knots to count days, lunar cycles, and other natural phenomena, usually to coordinate action among people who do not see each other frequently. Day cites examples from Herodotus, the Khond people of South Asia, and several indigenous groups in Africa, the Americas, and the Pacific Islands, in which knots in a cord were tied (or untied) to count the days until a next meeting—for a wedding, a battle, a feast, or some other social function. This method can be adapted to other sorts of counting as well, as in the example of a long and complex tax collector's cord seen in Hawaii in the early 19th century and recording the type, number, and location of items collected.[2]

This means of tallying seems to have reached its most sophisticated level of development in pre-Columbian Peru, where *quipus*, or groups of knotted cords, were used to record and calculate numerical data (taxes collected and owed, astronomical data, census information, for example) as well as cultural history and lore. The simplest form of quipu is a cord with many cords dangling from it. In more complex quipus, several cords are joined to a single dangling cord, making a group; in some cases, this group also includes a "summation" cord which tallies the information from the group. Numbers are recorded using a decimal system and in some cases these numbers reached into the tens of thousands (the Peruvian empire was a large and thriving at its height). Arriving Spaniards were astonished by the complexity and accuracy of this system, superior to that of their own accountants.[3]

The Luba people of Zaire, whose empire flourished in the 18th century and first half of the 19th century in Central Africa, had an elaborate mnemonic technology called *lukasa*, or memory boards. Measuring 20–25 centimeters long and about 13 centimeters wide, these carved boards had a slightly domed back carved in the style of the shell of the tortoise, the patron animal of the Luba. The front of the memory board (or "long hand") was studded with beads and carved bumps and ridges, each of which had symbolic significance. Beads were of different sizes and colors, and arranged singly or in clusters, according to a system codified by the ruling Bambudye, a secret society from which Luba leaders were exclusively drawn. Lukasa were the exclusive property of the Bambudye and their public narration of Luba lore and genealogy was supported and

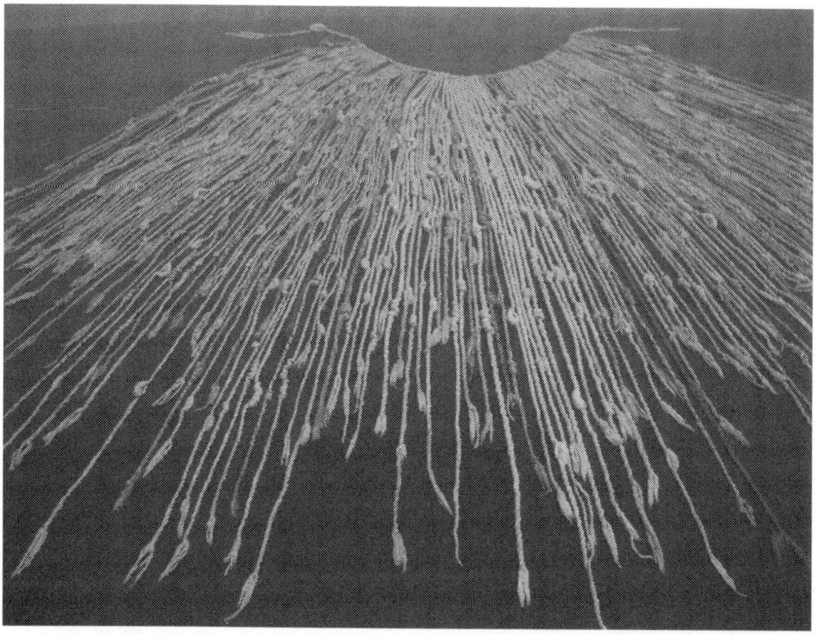

Figure 4.1 An antique quipu.

Figure 4.2 A modern reconstruction of some knots used in quipu.

prompted by the symbols on the lukasa. Reefe[4] reports that there were three sorts of lukasa: the first was an aid to retelling the elaborate origin story of the Luba empire, ensuring that the important protagonists and events would all be included in their proper order, despite individual variations in particular narrators' performance. The second type recorded extensive information on the organization of Bambudye society, including titles, functions, and patronage relationships. The third type contained secret information held by individual rulers; the specifics are likely lost to history.

> All memory boards, regardless of type, also record important cultural information such as the complexities of initiation rituals, codes of conduct such as an emphasis on mutual aid, and the names of deities and ancestral spirits as well as a notation on sacred spots. In a complex, [pre-literate] society, the lukasa were important supports for the ownership and recall of information important to social cohesion and the legitimation of power.[5]

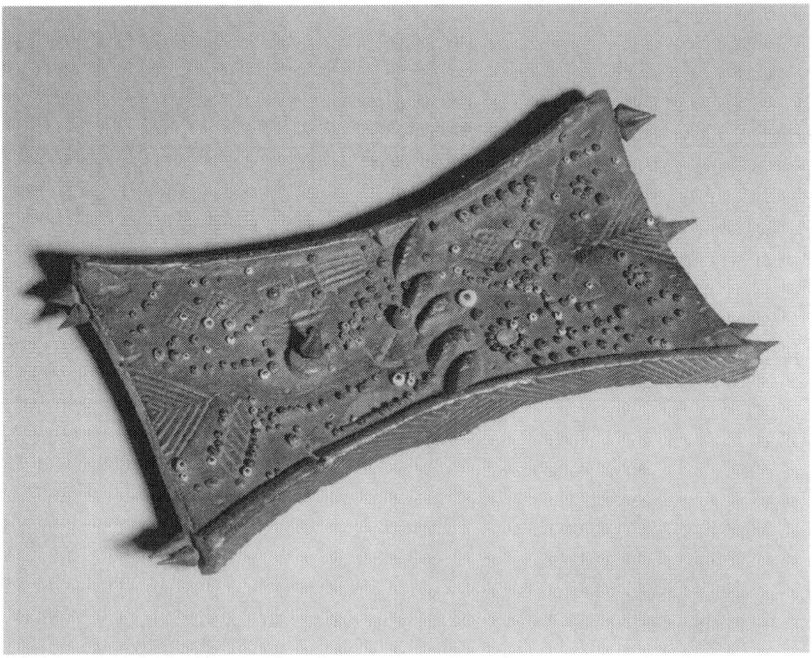

Figure 4.3 A lukasa memory board from the Luba people of central Africa.

In the Western cannon, many mnemonic techniques have been developed over time; perhaps the best known, which comes to us by way of ancient Greece, is the method of *loci*, or places. Cicero, writing about memory, which he considered one of the five parts of rhetoric, tells the story of Simonides of Ceos, who was called away from a banquet just before the roof of the banquet hall collapsed, killing all but Simonides. The bodies of the dead were so mangled that they could only be identified by their location, which Simonides was able to recall by the use of his well-developed memory (he had been hired to chant a long lyric poem praising his host, which he did from memory as was the custom). This is the "origin story" of the method of loci, which involves memorizing a space, then associating the items one wants to recall with different parts of the space. The memory palace and its cousin, the memory theater, are variants of this method. The memory palace is so called because to remember a long list of people, objects, or verses requires an elaborate space with many locations or rooms, and perhaps also with elaborate furnishings or architectural detail with which additional items can be associated and thus recalled. The person using this method must first commit to memory the details of the palace, real or imaginary, so that these details can be fluently recalled. Then the memorizer creates a mental association between these well-remembered features and the items that he or she wishes to recall. Retrieving the items involves a mental walk through the memory palace, plucking each item in turn from the location where it has been stored.[6] Today, with printed materials and search engines, information is stored and retrieved in a very different way, but the technique lives on in memory competitions such as the World Memory Championships[7] and in the Mind Palace that Sherlock Holmes uses in the BBC/Masterpiece television series starring actor Benedict Cumberbatch.[8]

Since the days of Simonides and Cicero there have been many variants of this method, including physical and graphic ways of presenting information to organize, store, and retrieve it. The "memory theater" of Renaissance scholar Giulio Camillo was a model theater made of wood, organized according to abstruse principles inspired by Vitruvius, Cicero, the Kabbala, and other systems of thought. Figure 4.4 sketches a rough breakdown of its organization but does not include reported features such as boxes or drawers to store works on paper. The theater was celebrated during Camillo's lifetime, and sponsored by patrons including the king of France, but few saw it during the life of the secretive creator.

In contrast, the "Temple of Time" by pioneering American educator Emma Willard, is a graphic representation of historical chronology. The chart shows two parallel rows of Greek columns, receding in pictorial

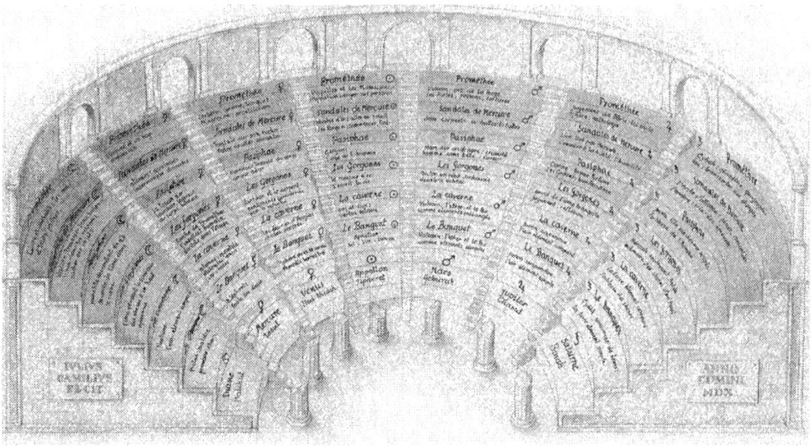

Figure 4.4 A 17th century rendering of Guilio Camillo's memory theater by Kircher.

perspective back to a rear wall labeled "The Creation," with more recent events arrayed along the columns in chronological order ending with the most recent. Developed by Willard in the early 19th century and used at the school she founded as well as by many other teachers, the Temple was intended as an aid to the study of history, deliberately analogous to the study of maps in geography class. Willard created a number of other graphic representations as well, with the goal of organizing information to promote and make more efficient the process of learning.[9]

Willard was quite explicit that her Temple of Time and other graphics were not intended just to aid memorization, but to support insight into connections between events, people, places, and eras. A published version from 1846 bears an inscription that includes the following:

> The attempt to understand chronology by merely committing dates to memory, is not only painful, but it is as useless as to learn latitudes and longitudes without the study of maps. As in geography, the relation of any place to all other places is what is important to know; so in chronology, the relation which any given event bears to others constitutes the only useful knowledge. . . . This saves great labor of thought, and may suggest new ideas, even to the learned.[10]

Willard sees objects and representations not just as facilitating memory but also as prompting new insights through juxtaposition and association.

Working Memory

We may also use objects of various kinds to help us "keep in mind" the elements of a complex project while we are at work on it. Writers typically use copious notes in order not to hold everything in their heads; fiction writers, for example, may use character sketches, plot timelines, and photographs of the novel's setting. In writing this book, I am using images, notes on index cards, an outline, concept maps, an online dictionary and thesaurus, file folders, files on a laptop, and evocative physical objects to support my writing process and to "keep in mind" what I want to say. That way I don't have to keep everything in my head, which would make for a very short book.

Some of the ways in which people offload cognition are quite simple and culturally widespread. Finger counting is commonly used by children to learn numbers, and to recall quantities during arithmetic operations. Some cultures have complex finger-counting systems that support more advanced operations and may continue to be used by adults (think abacus, but on your fingers; I discuss this further in Chapter 6). Studies of children with and without difficulties learning mathematics show that finger gnosia (the ability to perceive and recognize one's fingers, which some people lack) is highly correlated with elementary math performance, particularly on tasks where storage and manipulation of small magnitudes (numbers one through ten) is needed.[11] The ability to reduce demands on working memory by offloading to the fingers was more important than other factors in explaining the performance of the children studied.

Digital objects can be enormously helpful in supporting short term memory. In a study of designers working collaboratively on a room-design task,[12] teams using a digital tabletop touch-based interface, allowing multiple users to simultaneously use both hands to manipulate design images, were more effective than teams that used the conventional graphical user interface (a keyboard, screen, and mouse). Because the tabletop team could more readily "offload cognition" by storing multiple designs at their fingertips, rather than holding them in their heads, they were able to explore more alternatives and engage in more "problem-finding" and "re-representation." The result was deeper insight into the design problem and more creative solutions.

At my university, graduate students conducting qualitative research (research with primarily non-numerical data) have a new software tool which makes all their research notes, images, coding schemes, and interview transcripts more accessible and allows them, their fellow students, and their adviser unprecedented visibility into their project (see Interlude D for a description). The students create a new "object"—an electronic project—which captures the many elements of their evolving work. This serves both to offload cognition (less to "keep in mind") and to allow rapid movement among multiple representations of the student's research project.[13]

Chunking and Categorization

Grouping or categorizing can also reduce cognitive load and thus assist thinking. Psychologists have identified what they call "chunking," in which items are grouped with other items with which they have strong association. This is a cognitive process that can be conducted consciously and deliberately, as when we pack an overnight bag containing "things I will need for my trip" or we try to organize errands into geographic categories for an efficient shopping run. It can also happen automatically, during the process of perception, when we chunk things we have learned to associate with one another. When a neighbor gives me their home telephone number, I might recognize both the first three digits (the area code) and the next three digits (the exchange) as the same as my own phone number. Remembering familiar and meaningful groupings of digits, which are stored as a chunk, is far easier than recalling a random string of numbers. A classic article by psychologist George Miller, "The magical number seven, plus or minus two"[14] outlined the significant limits on what people can hold in memory. By grouping into chunks, we can "hold in mind" information of greater complexity.

Research evidence cites the superior ability of chess masters to recall positions of chess pieces on a board—even when the game had not been played by them and the examination of the board was only brief—as evidence for perceptual chunking. The chess masters' recall was far weaker but still superior to that of a non-chess player when the arrangement of the pieces was random. Researchers attribute this phenomenon to learned perceptual chunking, because recalling the location of an average of 25 pieces across 64 locations would be a truly remarkable feat for limited human memory. Masters' knowledge of chess moves and how an ensemble of chess pieces generally behaves allows data reduction by mapping the location of the pieces onto patterns of play, or chunks.[15]

A cliché or stereotype is a kind of chunk. Interestingly, these words were originally printer's terms, from the era of moveable type. A cliché was a commonly used phrase that a printer (or more likely their apprentice) could compose ahead of time, grabbing the entire phrase instead of each letter separately during the composition process. A stereotype similarly was a plate cast from an image or assembly of words or both; like the cliché, it speeded up and simplified the printing process. Stereotypes and clichés substitute convenience for originality, showing that chunking can introduce error and rigidity even while it provides blessed relief from cognitive overload.

In *Dreaming in Code*,[16] his account of three years in the life of an innovative software development project, author Scott Rosenberg describes the preparation for a meeting with funders, who will press to learn how soon they can expect to see a working version of the software. The team looks at a spreadsheet that lists features planned and the tasks associated with implementing that feature, but they can't get a good grip on their situation by looking at a giant spreadsheet. Their solution is to make a matrix of sticky notes on their whiteboard, where each note represents a month or two of the time of a single programmer. Some features require only one sticky note, others two or more. Then they arrange the notes on the whiteboard, categorized by how soon the feature will be implemented and which of the three major teams will be responsible for the task. Each sticky note is a "chunk" of tasks, but the details of the tasks are hidden or "black boxed" because at the moment the team is only interested in getting a sense of how long the overall project will take. By hiding the details the group can focus on the bigger picture, and can perform yet another level of chunking—organizing the stickies into groups, or chunks, that show which development team (apps, services, or repository) is responsible for the tasks. In this way, the team creates a physical instantiation of the project plan and reduces cognitive load for the project team by chunking a large and complex set of tasks and offloading cognition to the display on the whiteboard.

When a student practices a cognitive or motor skill repeatedly, the sequence of thoughts or actions can become a sort of chunk, more easily stored and more easily retrieved. Instead of the need to consciously recall and implement each step of a process—whether the sequence of a chess game or a cello sonata, the detailed movements of a competitive figure skater, or the diagnostic ability of a doctor—actions and reasoning become more automatic and therefore less demanding of the limited bandwidth we have for conscious thought.[17]

Support for Spatial Thinking

In education, when we emphasize the development of basic skills in young people we stress language (both reading and writing) and mathematics in particular. Yet there is another basic skill, perhaps unseen precisely because it is so fundamental, and that is the skill of spatial thinking. Our bodies exist in space and encounter it constantly, from birth and even before (the womb, of course, is a space, and parents know that babies are active well before they emerge into the wider world). The developing child is constantly exploring, and these explorations always take place *in space*, because that is where we live and where we embodied thinkers do our thinking. We learn to perceive, to reason about, and to act in and with space as we grow, and these abilities are essential to our survival as individuals and to the survival of our species (think hunting, planting, searching for food and shelter, let alone all the daily activities of life in more developed societies).

In its report, *Learning to Think Spatially*, the National Research Council offers a description of its target subject.

> Spatial thinking—one form of thinking—is based on a constructive amalgam of three elements: concepts of space, tools of representation, and processes of reasoning. It is the concept of space that makes spatial thinking a distinctive form of thinking. By understanding the meaning of space, we can use its properties (e.g., dimensionality, continuity, proximity, and separation) as a vehicle for structuring problems, for finding answers, and for expressing solutions.[18]

Paradoxically, the ubiquity of human spatial thinking makes it easy to overlook. It's the foundation of our functioning, and often comes to our attention only when there is a breakdown of some sort. When a child has motor problems, or an engineering student can't understand a blueprint, or an athlete keeps missing the mark, our attention is called to the need for spatial thinking. Yet we are always thinking spatially, in ways large and small, when we walk across the room, prepare a meal, rearrange furniture, plan a route to work, pack a suitcase or the trunk of the car, and a nearly infinite list of everyday activities. It is the foundation of mnemonic methods such as the memory palace. Spatial thinking is found in more specialized forms in the disciplines, and learning to think spatially is fundamental to many areas of science, mathematics, the arts, as well as many blue- and pink-collar areas of work like the building trades and health care.

Spatial thinking can be key to new insights. Famous examples include Watson and Crick's discovery of the structure of the DNA molecule (and accounts of the race to solve this vexing scientific problem mention that they built a large physical model of DNA, shown in Figure B.3.) Chemist August Wilhelm Kekulé had a strong interest in architecture, and his orientation toward thinking spatially about molecules contributed to his breakthrough insights about the structure of the benzene ring, helping to launch the field of organic chemistry.[19] Physician John Snow is celebrated for his map showing the link between cholera outbreaks and the location of public water pumps (with their differential water sources) in mid-19th century London, a breakthrough in public health that helped to launch the field of epidemiology.[20]

Harvard astrophysicist and MacArthur Prize Fellow Margaret Geller attributed her important insights that galaxies are not distributed evenly across the universe to her early training in spatial thinking. Her father, a crystallographer at Bell Labs, brought home with him "any kind of toy that had anything to do with geometry."

> He'd explain to me the relationship between things that I built and things in the world. For example, I'd make a cube, and he'd explain to me the relationship between that and the structure of table salt. And I'd make an icosahedron, and he'd explain how you see that in the real world. He would talk about filling space and which figures could fill space and which couldn't. . . . He would say things—this structure was this or that—and he'd show me the beautiful models of the crystal structures, and I wouldn't be able to see it. But he would say it again and again and again. And finally, I would be able to see those spatial relations.[21]

"I realize now," she said, "I've talked to lots of people in science—that very few people have that [spatial] ability."[22]

The National Research Council[23] highlights both the fundamental importance of spatial thinking and the relative neglect of spatial thinking in the school curriculum. Few children have father's like Geller's, and the ability to perceive, represent, and reason about space is often taken for granted. As a result, spatial thinking is often not taught, and students' deficits in the ability to think spatially may go unnoticed—or be spotted in college engineering, science, or health classes, at a point where there may be no remedial help available and students simply wash out of the major.

I have seen some evidence in my own classroom of spatial thinking deficits. Unlike most social science professors, I have students in my general education classes make physical things. In addition to short exercises with Lego, clay, and other materials, I assign a project on which students work during the second half of the term. Instead of the usual term paper, which both my students and I often find deadly, I have them choose a project on a significant topic relevant to the class. Their deliverables at the end of the semester are a poster, explaining their project in text and images; an "elevator pitch" which is the basis for the brief conversations they will have with visitors during the project open house at the end of the semester; and an "artifact" that expresses some aspect of their project in three dimensional terms. (See Interlude E for a more extended description.)

In a course on sustainable development I remember a pair of young women who got interested in geothermal energy and built a model house complete with a microprocessor-based thermostat of their own design. They sensibly hung a model fan from the ceiling of the single-room house to recirculate hot air. The fan was fashioned from two tongue depressors laid crosswise. When I suggested to them that such a crude fan was not in keeping with the elegant detail of other parts of their house and that they find something more like the propeller of a model airplane they looked baffled. It turned out that they had never noticed that the blades of a fan were tilted rather than flat; this prevented them from reasoning, for example, about how and why air is pushed by a fan. Although the final version of their house retained the tongue depressor fan, barely visible in the picture of their project in Figure 4.5, they added a very effective small fan contraption

Figure 4.5 My students' model geothermal house with an improved fan, showing their spatial learning.

to the floor of their house, where it could blow cool air up from the basement, where they had placed an ice pack. In this way the students were able to demonstrate their spatial learning as well as their learning of other principles, like feedback, at the heart of a device like a thermostat.

Spatial thinking is complex and has many components:

> To think spatially entails knowing about (1) space—for example, different ways of calculating distance (e.g., in miles, in travel time, in travel cost), the basis of coordinate systems (e.g., Cartesian versus polar coordinates), and the nature of spaces (e.g., in terms of the number of dimensions [two versus three]); (2) representation—for example, the relationships among views (e.g., plans versus elevations of buildings, orthogonal versus perspective maps), the effect of projections (e.g., Mercator versus equal-area map projections), and the principles of graphic design (e.g., the roles of legibility, visual contrast, and figure-ground organization in the readability of graphs and maps); and (3) reasoning—for example, the different ways of thinking about shortest distances (e.g., as the crow flies versus route distance in a rectangular street grid), the ability to extrapolate and interpolate (e.g., projecting a functional relationship on a graph into the future, estimating the slope of a hillside from a map of contour lines), and making decisions (e.g., given traffic reports on a radio, selecting a detour).[24]

These skills, no matter how sophisticated, have as their foundation the embodied experience of the learner from the very first hours of life. This experience in three-dimensional space lays the groundwork for future learning of both simple daily skills and abstractions like language and mathematics. I was alarmed to learn, in a recent conversation with a preschool teacher, that she has students who can use a block-stacking app on an iPad but can't easily stack actual blocks in her classroom. I fear that we are creating a generation of students who can't notice that fan blades are tilted; what else will they be missing about the physical world we inhabit?

One matter of concern to educators is group and individual differences in spatial ability. Professors may assume a given level of spatial skill in their students, but if individuals are weak in some areas they will have a more difficult time learning the material. Furthermore, if some demographic groups have a higher proportion of members with weak spatial skills, these groups may be systematically discouraged from pursuing further education in a field that presumes particular spatial skills. In engineering, many faculty members believe that women have weaker spatial skills than men, and some colleges, in an attempt to retain otherwise-qualified students, offer remedial spatial training. As Margaret Geller's experience with her father's tutelage demonstrates, spatial ability can be encouraged and improved for all students under favorable conditions. Whether my students' spatial perception overall was improved by my instruction I do not know, but I'm pretty confident that they did not look at a ceiling fan the same way again.

Inquiry and Interaction

Inquiry and interaction are fundamental to learning, and "things to think with" play a central role as fodder for inquiry. These things need not be physical, but material objects have many characteristics that make them good to think with. In addition to their mnemonic functions and their spatial qualities, discussed earlier, they can also be observed, manipulated, and reconfigured, and by "talking back" can prompt discovery and cause learners to think in a new way. By moving, juxtaposing, manipulating, and evaluating an object or a combination of objects, new features and opportunities may come to light. Recall that Levi-Strauss, in exploring how "primitive" man's thinking with things could have led in time to the Neolithic revolution in human material culture—the development of weaving, pottery, and the domestication of plants and animals, for example—called these human activities of sustained observation and experimentation a "science of the concrete." As we saw in Chapter 2, Levi-Strauss describes an interactive inquiry into the characteristics of natural and man-made objects and an exploration of how they might be useful, analogous to today's "tinkerer" who may start with a finite set of materials, perhaps cast-offs collected seemingly at random, and assemble them through the gradual experimentation of *bricolage* into a useful system.

In the 21st century, scholar of creativity and education Anna Craft has asserted that "at the heart of all creativity is possibility thinking." And at the heart of possibility thinking lie two questions: "What does this do?" and "What can I do with this?"[25] The first question favors exploration of an object or situation on its own terms, so as to understand its affordances and constraints. The second question brings the thinker's own purposes and context into the mix, asking how I can take the features of what I have before me and turn it to my own ends. These questions, it seems to me, are fundamental to deep learning as well as to creativity, and they are already present in Levi-Strauss' "primitive" thinker.

Bamberger and Schön call Levi-Strauss' dialogue a "conversation with materials" that facilitates learning and meaning making through coming "to see in a new way."[26] In one study, they observed pairs of musically untrained adults working with a set of five Montessori bells (all of which looked identical but each of which had a different pitch). The pair were asked to "make a tune that you like using all the bells in the collection."[27] In the process of constructing a tune the participants rang the bells, discussed them, and rearranged them, now in one configuration (such as a pleasing sequence) and then in another (like low to high pitch). Using careful analysis of videotapes:

> We found our participants improvising; we found them engaged in on-the-spot experimenting in response to the new phenomena they were discovering. In short, we found them "conversing" with their materials. . . . [We observed] the gradual evolution of making something through reflective "conversation" between makers and their materials in the course of shaping meaning and coherence. "Reflective" has at least two intentions here . . . [which] can be thought of as two kinds of "talking back." In the first, the makers talk back to the materials (reshaping them); in the second, the materials talk back to the makers, re-shaping what the makers know about them." Unexpected insight evolves in the work of making, but makers tend only to see it when, *through the evolutionary process of the making, itself,* they can recognize it.[28]

This emphasis on inquiry and interaction was central to the work of John Dewey as well.

At the Bauhaus, the famed German design school of the early 20th century, entering students first took the *Vorkurs*, a preliminary one-term course of study with three main purposes: first, to free students from the "dead wood of convention"[29] and enable them to create their own original work; second, by experimenting with a wide range of materials, to allow the student to discover the material to which he or she was most drawn—wood, glass, metal, textiles, and so forth. Finally, to teach students principles of form, color, and composition that would be the basis for their evolving work. Johannes Itten, originator of the *Vorkurs*, gave his students exercises in monochromatic contrast such as creating both a white and a black circle (not as easy as it sounds) and creating an array of subtly different tones; other exercises might involve creating a composition juxtaposing found materials of different textures, or experimenting with various sorts of color contrast. To use Anna Craft's framing, Itten took students from "what does this do?"

to "what can I do with this?" in the course of a semester. Inquiry and interaction were at the heart of his teaching.

An important aspect of all things to think with are their "affordances."[30] An object's affordances are those things that the object's features supports: a pen affords writing but not drinking, a mug affords drinking but not writing. Through their affordances, objects steer our attention in some directions and not others. A telescope affords looking at distant objects and seeing them as if they were close; a patchwork quilt affords warmth and comfort, and can provoke thoughts about the lives of people in previous generations.

Affordance's flip side, constraint, is equally valuable, because by narrowing possibility it aids focus and prompts novel problem-solving. The Froebel Kindergarten materials afford playful experimentation and inquiry—childhood *bricolage*—within a structure of constraints. Accomplished artists and designers also recognize the centrality of constraints to creative work. Composer Igor Stravinsky wrote explicitly about this.

> My freedom thus consists in my moving about within the narrow frame that I have assigned myself for each one of my undertakings. . . . Whatever diminishes constraint, diminishes strength. The more constraints one imposes, the more one frees one's self of the chains that shackle the spirit.[31]

Celebrated modern designer Charles Eames said,

> Design depends largely on constraints. . . . Here is one of the few effective keys to the design problem—the ability of the designer to recognize as many of the constraints as possible—his willingness and enthusiasm for working within these constraints. Constraints of price, of size, of strength, of balance, of surface, of time, and so forth.[32]

Even in the arcane world of software development, "Constraints are key to building a great product," according to a very successful software entrepreneur. "They're what makes creativity happen. If someone said you have all the money in the world to build whatever you want, it would probably never be released."[33]

Evocation

We respond to objects not just rationally, but also emotionally (and, as Chapter 2 discussed, reason and emotion are inseparable in any case). Sherry

Turkle's phrase "evocative objects" highlights the "inseparability of thought and feeling in our relationship to things."[34] For each of us, there are objects we find particularly resonant and important, and which may have particular staying power over the course of a lifetime. In short essays collected by Turkle, writers discuss a selected object that for them has been particularly evocative. The objects range from knots to stars, from a glucometer to slime mold, and from a train in the Australian outback to Foucault's pendulum. Each has deep and individual meaning for the writer, and each is a *thing to think (and feel) with*, a sort of touchstone that captures some key essence.

English pediatrician and psychoanalyst D. W. Winnicott writes about the central importance of a "transitional object" in infant development. At first, an infant is unable to perceive their primary caregiver as separate from themselves. As the separateness of the primary caregiver begins to dawn on the infant, a transitional object, often something like a blanket or stuffed toy, can help to bridge the potentially terrifying gulf between self and other. The transitional object is under the child's control, more or less, while a parent, even a doting one, is not. The transitional object provides comfort and security because of the child's sense of control and the constancy of the object (think Linus and his blanket from the comic strip *Peanuts*). While transitional objects and evocative objects are not synonymous, they surely rhyme. Turkle writes that Winnicott believed that throughout life we continue to seek "objects we can experience as both within and outside the self."[35]

Meaning-Making and Metaphor

An important way in which we use things is in the process of meaning-making. This is an ongoing human activity, operating constantly and often unconsciously, to the point that we often don't realize that we are always engaged in meaning making. Sometimes a problem or an object will bring us up short, causing us to consciously stop and think, but most of the time we are assessing the nature and significance of our environment simply as a part of daily living. What is that coming toward us? Friend or foe or machine? What's on my desk and what does it require of me? Why did my colleague/student/spouse do that? Meaning making is the work of philosophers, painters, physicists, and psychologists, but it is also a task of everyday living.

The things around us, our environment, our "situation" as John Dewey would have it, are some of the raw materials on which we draw to construct meaning. Even more important are the internal resources on the basis of which individuals construct meaning. In *The Meaning of the Body*, philosopher Mark Johnson challenges the dominant philosophical view of meaning in the 20th century: meaning as a disembodied and decontextualized set of propositions about the world. Instead, Johnson argues,

> meaning grows from our visceral connections to life and the bodily conditions of life . . . it is through our bodily perceptions, movements, emotions, and feelings that meaning becomes possible . . . meaning is not just a matter of concepts and propositions, but also reaches down into the images, sensorimotor schemas, feelings, qualities, and emotions that constitute our meaningful encounter with our world.[36]

In this view, meaning can be enhanced and further developed through the use of language, but can also exist independent of language, and even in a form that cannot readily be expressed in language. Indeed, in their classic book, *Metaphors We Live By*,[37] Johnson and his co-author, linguist George Lakoff, argue convincingly for the view that metaphors are not just ornaments of linguistic expression but reflect fundamental aspects of our worldview. They unpack everyday metaphors to show how ubiquitous they are, and how they shape our views about, and actions toward, the things described. When talking about arguments we may use metaphors of war ("your position is indefensible" or "I demolished him in front of his boss"); of spatial orientation when discussing moods ("I'm feeling up today" or "don't let the bastards get you down"); and ideas may be buildings ("her theory is without foundation") or people ("he is the father of epidemiology") or commodities ("she won't buy that approach"). These metaphors affect how we view particular situations, and thus how we choose to act toward them.

Psychologist of art Rudolf Arnheim describes the embodied, kinesthetic experience of metaphor:

> Gestures will act out the pursuit of an argument as though it were a prize fight, showing the weighing of alternatives, the tug of war, the subtle attack, the crushing impact of the victorious retort. This spontaneous use of metaphor demonstrates not only that human beings are naturally aware of the structural resemblance uniting physical and non-physical objects and events; one must go further and assert that the perceptual qualities of shape and motion are present in the very acts of thinking depicted by the gestures and are in fact the medium in which the thinking itself takes place. These perceptual qualities are

> not necessarily visual or only visual. In gestures, the kinesthetic experiences of pushing, pulling, advancing, obstructing, are likely to play an important part.[38]

"*The essence of metaphor*," say Lakoff and Johnson, "*is understanding and experiencing one kind of thing in terms of another*."[39] Donald Schön calls this "seeing-as" and draws our attention to the way in which some metaphors—generative metaphor, in his terminology—can be essential aids to innovation and problem-solving. He describes a group of product engineers puzzling over a new paintbrush with synthetic bristles. The synthetic paintbrush was not performing well—"gloppy" was one word used to describe how it delivered paint—and the engineers had tried various strategies to make the new brush's performance comparable to that of natural bristle brushes. The breakthrough came when one engineer mused, "You know, a paintbrush is a kind of pump!"[40] By seeing a paintbrush as a pump, the engineers moved their focus from the bristles themselves to the channels between the bristles and how the paint flowed through the channels. The paintbrush-as-pump metaphor was generative in the sense that it led to a new way of seeing the problem, and this new framing generated a new and successful solution. This is one very powerful form of human meaning-making.

When we describe the university as an "ivory tower," we are seeing the academy as something both precious and removed. Although the phrase originated as a term of praise in the biblical Song of Solomon, today it is often used to disparage the university as a site of privilege, disconnected from the concerns of everyday people. That disconnection has some significant benefits, allowing professors and students to pursue important, interesting, and unpopular questions that have no immediate or guaranteed payoff; it also can result in thinking that is not grounded in the outside world or in societal benefit.

Alternatively, the academy is a "marketplace of ideas." This metaphor for the university shifts our focus in the opposite direction: toward trade, an assessment of value, an economic model. The scrum of the bazaar grounds the academy, replacing the lofty aloofness of the ivory tower, but also appears to threaten what makes the university special and apart. The battle between these two views has played out over the last century and more in American higher education.[41] These metaphors capture succinctly the views of some combatants about what is at stake, and serve as shorthand for complex ideas. They guide and limit debate. Metaphors have consequences.

When students in my classroom build, they are making meaning and even metaphor. I ask my students to spend five minutes building with Lego in order to respond to a question I pose them. Prompts I have used include: "What are the qualities of your ideal study environment?," "Think of a person, place, or thing that has influenced your life and build something that will help you tell us about it," or "Who will you be five years from now?" What students build is sometimes a literal model (their bedroom, their desk, a bench under a tree) but often it is metaphorical to some extent. Students build things that have elements of an airplane to express their aspiration to rise to new heights, or of a car to reflect their desire to experience the wider world, or of the natural world to show their interest in growth and flourishing.

I often introduce this exercise on the first day of class. After students build, we go around the room, and each student briefly tells what they built and what it means. The metaphors students use succinctly capture something that would take much longer to express in words, and that might even be more threatening to reveal in explicit statements to classmates. Lego constructions, because they exist outside of the self, and because they are playful, allow students to connect with deeper emotions and project them onto their constructions. Students may reveal emotional states like depression and anxiety as they describe their constructions; it is unlikely that they would mention these as part of the standard verbal self-introduction in a new class. An exercise like this takes us beyond the introduction basics of name, major, and year in school, accelerating the process of getting to know my students.

An important feature of the Lego task is that it must be done quickly, with a minimum of conscious planning. "Don't overthink this. Dive in!" I tell students who are hesitating. Just get started. Their constructions, then, are emergent. As students build, they think of new features to add, or discover new affordances or constraints in the Lego set, or may have an idea that pops into their head as they see something new in what they have built. They are actively making and modifying meaning as they build, often discovering things about themselves along the way. Even students who have used Lego before have not used them in this way, and the novel activity in which they are engaged may lead them to generative metaphors. They are constructing an understanding as they construct their Lego responses. This is construct*ionism*, an enhancement of the widely accepted learning theory construct*ivism*, which holds that students construct new knowledge by building on the structure and foundation of their existing knowledge. Constructionism "adds the idea that this happens especially felicitously in a context where the learner is consciously engaged in constructing a public entity, whether it's a sand castle on the beach or a theory of the universe."[42]

Even when students are not making metaphor, they are still making meaning. Children making patterns with Froebel blocks, even when these patterns are not explicitly representational, are making meaning, even if that meaning is impossible for the child to articulate. Indeed, young children—and many adults too—may be far more articulate in their making than they are able to be in language. Rudolf Arnheim points to the importance of the patterns human beings make,

> Every visual pattern—be it that of a painting, a building, an ornament, a chair—can be considered a proposition which, more or less successfully, makes a declaration about the nature of human existence . . . any organized pattern is a carrier of meaning, whether intended or not.[43]

Imaginative Projection

It's even possible to think with a thing that is not, and cannot, be held in the hand. Two celebrated cases of scientific breakthrough are of this sort. At age 15, Albert Einstein was so unhappy with the rote learning and regimentation at his German high school that he left school with the plan to study on his own for the entrance examinations for the technical college in Zurich. Although he was younger than the required age he was allowed to sit for the exams, easily passing the mathematics and science section but failing the general section, which included literature, biology, politics, and French language. On the advice of the college's director, Einstein enrolled for a year of remedial work at a nearby school in Aarau. It was a very happy year for him. The teaching methods were based on the work of Pestalozzi, Froebel's mentor and inspiration, and encouraged students to closely observe, conceptualize, and visualize while forming their own conclusions. The opposite of the approach that has so antagonized Einstein in high school, the school in Aarau placed a priority on visual understanding, with language and computation secondary. Einstein had been slow to use language as a child, and continued to struggle with French (it was his lowest mark when he passed the Zurich Polytechnic exams at the end of the year) but the encouragement to visualize and to perform thought experiments fit perfectly with his strengths and his inclinations. It was at age 16, while attending the Aarau school, that Einstein first performed one of the feats of visual imagination for which he is best known—he imagined himself riding beside a beam of light as it coursed through space, examining its structure and behavior. It would be another decade before this thought experiment resulted in his formulation of the theory of special relativity, but the reinforcement the Aarau school gave him for his inclination to visualization and independent though was crucial. Constructed on a foundation of observing and reasoning about physical things in his environment, Einstein and his fellow students were able to use their grasp of what they observed to project themselves in their imagination into situations that could not be directly experienced or observed.[44]

While Einstein used his powers of imaginative projection to think about natural phenomena at the scale of the universe, his fellow Nobel Laureate Barbara McClintock used the same powers of imagination and empathy to make discoveries at a microscopic scale.[45] Her deep and immersive study of genetics and cytology over many decades led her to see what others were missing. Shortly after her election to the National Academy of Sciences, the most prestigious professional society in the US, McClintock made a visit to Stanford. Looking through the microscope there at the behavior of the chromosomes in a strain of fungi, McClintock was at first frustrated and unable to perceive what was going on. Feeling some desperation and a waning self-confidence, she took a break under the eucalyptus trees that line the campus drive. A sudden sense that it would all work out sent her back to the lab, and she was able to see what had looked simply like disorder an hour before.

> I found that the more I worked with [the chromosomes] the bigger and bigger [they] got, and when I was really working with them I wasn't outside, I was down there. I was part of the system . . . everything got big. I even was able to see the internal parts of the chromosomes. . . . It surprised me because I actually felt as if I were right down there and these were my friends.[46]

Her extraordinary ability to imaginatively project herself into the world of microscopic genes provided the insight to recognize what was thought to be impossible: that genetic material, rather than being fixed along a chromosome, could sometimes move position—even transposing to another chromosome—under the right conditions. Her immersive interaction with the genetics of the maize plant, her "feeling for the organism,"[47] led to extraordinary breakthroughs that were eventually recognized with a Nobel prize in Physiology or Medicine in 1983.

This ability to project oneself into a phenomenon of interest, and in so doing develop key insights, is not limited to Einstein and McClintock. Indeed, many scientists and others describe this as a part of their process. Nobel laureates including Richard Feynman, who wondered "If I were an electron, what would I do?" and astrophysicists Subrahmanyan Chandrasekhar and Hannes Alfven, who tried to imagine the universe from the point of view of a star or an ion, are "thinking with things" that they cannot touch, but which nevertheless have become for them like familiar friends.[48]

Imaginative projection is not just the province of gifted scientists, but can be part of the learning process for students of any age. We have already discussed the ways in which the methods of Froebel and his mentor Pestalozzi supported visualization and imagination; many other educators have encouraged a personal and embodied engagement with subjects like mathematics, which are often taught in the rote and regimented way that so irritated Einstein. In the 19th century, educator and theologian Edwin Abbott wrote the classic *Flatland*[49] in which the characters are geometric shapes who live in worlds of varying dimensionality. The narrator is a square in a two-dimensional world, where all other characters look like either lines (seen from the side) or points (line segments seen end-on). When he travels to a three-dimensional world, suddenly he sees that what looked to him like a line, or a circle, is actually a sphere, and so forth. Written as a social satire of Victorian mores and the class system, it is also an extended exercise in learning geometry from the point of view of geometric figures.

Mathematician and educator Seymour Papert developed Logo, a simple programming language, and a mechanical "turtle" that could be commanded using Logo. The turtle, a simple wheeled robot tethered to a computer, could be instructed to go forward and backward, and to turn, with distance and angle specified in the Logo program. Young students could learn "turtle geometry" by commanding the turtle, sometimes after working out how they wanted the turtle to move by going through the motions themselves. How to have the turtle make a circle? First walk in a circle yourself and figure out what it is you are doing, then put it in a symbolic language the turtle "understands." Papert uses the word "syntonic" to describe the congruence the child experiences between the body and the turtle, or the self and the turtle.[50] This congruence helps the child to make sense of mathematics, and to identify with the subject.

After a time, the turtle evolved to be an onscreen cursor controlled by Logo, so that the physical robot disappeared but a virtual representation remained. Interestingly, children who can relate in a physical, embodied way to the virtual turtle foreshadow the experience of professional programmers and computer chip designers who describe the (imaginative) experience of walking around inside their code or designs. Like geneticist Barbara McClintock, they are so familiar with the code on which they are working that they can imaginatively project themselves "down there" among the lines of symbols. Acts of imagination like this are often not "just" visual but also embodied. Einstein famously described his way of thinking as having nothing to do with language, but instead as visual and "muscular" or somatosensory.[51]

Social Thinking With Things

So far in this chapter we have been looking at how individuals use things in their thinking, but things are also useful for groups to think with. Although there is considerable overlap in how individuals and groups think with things, there are a few ways in which pairs and groups use things that are worth noting.

Instruction

A variety of physical materials are commonly used in instructional settings. They perform a range of functions, and their effectiveness has in part to do with how well they are suited to the topic and to the learner. Also important is how the instructor uses the materials with the student.

Wood, Bruner, and Ross[52] studied the interaction of an adult tutor with individual students ages 3 to 5 years old. The children were given a set of specially designed interlocking blocks that were to be assembled into a simple block pyramid. The job of the tutor was to closely observe the child as he or she manipulated the blocks, prompting the child in a gentle way as needed to guide them toward the goal.

After careful review of video recordings of thirty children interacting with the tutor, the authors identified six primary functions performed by the tutor as she guided the children.

Recruitment—capture the interest of the child and ensure that they follow the rules for the task.

Reduction in degrees of freedom—reduce the complexity of the task so that it is at a manageable level for the child's abilities and developmental stage.

Direction maintenance—keep the child pointed more or less toward the goal of the task.

Marking critical features—point out important features of the materials or the task that the child may have overlooked, and noting discrepancies between what the child has produced and what the task requires.

Frustration control—"Problem-solving should be less dangerous or stressful with a tutor than without."[53]

Demonstration—model solutions to the task, perhaps even performing for the child an improved version of an action the child has already taken.

Wood, Bruner, and Ross call these actions "scaffolding functions," using the metaphor of the scaffold which assists a building crew to reach places they could not reach with their body alone. The instructor is bringing the task to within the child's reach, enabling a child to take the next step toward accomplishing the goal. Like training wheels on a bicycle or a flotation device for a beginning swimmer, the tutor assists the child to grasp new things that would previously have been just out of reach. (Vygotsky calls this the "Zone of Proximal Development"[54]—the area that represents the difference between what the child can do unaided and what he or she can do with a tutor.) The word *scaffolding* is now in wide use among educators, and the construction metaphor it invokes both encourages and reinforces "constructivist" notions of learning. As is often the case, John Dewey said it first:

> It is . . . essential that the new objects and events be related intellectually to those of earlier experiences, and this means that there be some advance made in conscious articulation of facts and ideas. It thus becomes the office of the educator to select those things within the range of existing experience that have the promise and potentiality of presenting new problems which by stimulating new ways of observation and judgment will expand the area of further experience.[55]

While tutoring and scaffolding can certainly be done without material aids, it is worth noting the important functions that tangible materials play in this careful investigation of the scaffolding function. In the Wood, Bruner, and Ross study, enticing material—wooden blocks sized for children's hands and arrayed on a table in front of them—help to recruit the child's interest in the task. The blocks also, because they are specially designed to interlock in a particular way conducive to the construction of a pyramid, constrain the task and reduce the degrees of freedom available to the child—although not enough to enable all but the most capable 5-year-olds to complete the task unaided. This feature can also potentially help the child maintain direction toward the goal. The design of the blocks, with their small cylindrical pins and holes, also announce to the receptive viewer some of their critical features, although tutorial help is generally needed by the children. Finally, demonstration by an instructor can be most effective when there is something to demonstrate *with*—in this case the blocks. In addition to the verbal prompts that often sufficed for the 5-year-olds, the tutor was able to take pairs of blocks and show how they fit together, supplementing language with visual and manual cues.

Because it is the task of the tutor to observe the child and identify helpful interventions, the physical materials of the task can help to make the child's thinking visible to the instructor. Because the child is reasoning with materials, errors in strategy and problems envisioning the final product become more apparent. This ability of materials to make thinking visible helps the tutor to note more easily where the learner is "stuck," and affords physical demonstration, not just prompts with language.

The story of my first use of Lego in my Sustainable Development class, mentioned in Chapter 1, illustrates the way in which physical materials have been valuable to me in making the thinking of my students clear. While it's true that their lack of understanding could have come out in discussion, or on a quiz, the Lego task was a very quick, efficient, and engaging way to the dismaying conclusion that my students had not learned much from what they had been exposed to in that section of the class. The physical materials also made it easy and quick to model a better solution.

A second example, from a class some years later, is also worth recounting. In an undergraduate general education course, I had one student who never spoke and looked very disengaged. He came to class, but did not participate or react to what was going on in the room. About midway through the semester I introduced a Lego exercise that involved three quick building challenges. The first was a warmup—typically I ask students to build a tower, or a monument, or a garden, just to get them moving quickly and imaginatively with the Lego bricks. For the second challenge, the prompt was "Build a model of the one thing (or person) you would most like to have in your personal learning environment." While other students built things like trees or their bed or a pet, my seemingly disengaged student built an oddly abstract construction, shown in Figure 4.6. As we went around the room, with each student telling the class what they had built, we came to the silent student. He said, and I can remember it almost verbatim, "I need reflection. I come to class and I listen and take it all in, but I don't really

Figure 4.6 My student's Lego construction illustrated reflection.

learn it until I'm driving home and I replay the class in my head." It was a big lesson for me—do not assume you know what a student is thinking based simply on appearance. I was so glad that Lego had allowed me to learn about how he was processing the class.

In my Lego challenges to students, and in the experiments of Wood, Bruner, and Ross, there is an interesting tension. On the one hand, we give our learners a goal; on the other hand, a certain amount of manipulation of the materials, of "trying-out," is also valuable to the learner. That is why I start my series of Lego challenges with an extremely open-ended instruction, such as build a tower. Almost anything can be a tower if you say it is, and it gives the students five minutes to experiment with the bricks (and to find, for example, that Lego is not particularly well suited to the construction of tall slender things—such structures often fall down.) When I tell the students not to overthink and encourage them to start building even when they don't have a full plan in mind, I am echoing Wood, Bruner, and Ross, who started each session with a child and a tutor by allowing the child five minutes of free play with the materials. This beginning, and subsequent experimentation with the materials by the child, are just as important as having a clear goal in mind and working methodically toward that goal. There is a tension in both these settings—the Lego and the block pyramid task—between the top-down goal set by the instructor, and the inductive tinkering or bricolage of the student. Yet I would argue that this is a productive tension, which needs to be managed by the tutor or instructor as well as by the learner. Instead of being seen as a flawed process, the vacillation between experimentation and goal directed activity is an important part of constructing new knowledge. Physical materials help to make thinking visible and, in so doing, can aid demonstration and support mentoring.

One of the most universal, yet also underutilized in formal education, things to think with in instruction is the body. Around the world we teach children to count on their fingers, and here the "material" used needs no introduction. Our bodies are perhaps the most familiar thing to think with, and always "ready to hand." A therapist was working with a boy who could not do simple arithmetic and found that using his body to teach him was powerfully effective.

> He had no idea what numbers mean. He had no feeling or understanding of what counting is. . . . Where's the easiest place to find that out? It's your own body. As soon as we did it with movements, he understood it.[56]

Fingers, and the body, can be a great scaffold for mathematics instruction. In fact, mathematics arguably originates in the embodied mind.[57]

A more elaborate example of instruction with things comes from my undergraduate general education course, "Designing the Future World" (described in Interlude E.) Beginning mid-semester, students work in pairs to select an important social, environmental, or economic issue (most complex problems can have elements of all three) and create a project that proposes a product or intervention that could help move the current state of the problem in a positive direction. Over the remaining weeks of the semester, students give a five-minute slide presentation of their idea to the class for critique, show a draft of the poster they will be presenting on the last day of class, make a mock up or "concept prototype" of an artifact that dramatizes or demonstrates their project, and deliver a one-minute "elevator pitch" about their project. These elements come together on the final day of class, when students set up their posters and artifacts in the classroom or a more public space. Visitors drop in to see and discuss the projects during this open house, giving students feedback about their work. Examples of student projects include remote-control roving devices with sensors that can detect and map pollution; a handheld device to read product bar codes and report on the environmental and social performance of the manufacturer; and a proposal to put the anti-overdose medication Narcan in glass boxes like those that house fire extinguishers and defibrillators in public buildings.

The six tutoring functions described by Wood, Bruner, and Ross earlier also apply to my work with students and their projects. First, the opportunity to do a project on a topic they have chosen, and especially to do something that has a physical and public incarnation, is engaging to the students. Every semester, at least one student tells me how refreshing it is not to have to write yet another term paper, and the fact that they choose a topic they find important, and prepare for a public "performance" of their work, is energizing for the vast majority of students. Second, I reduce the degrees of freedom for the task by telling students that they should not expect to generate a *solution* for a complex, open ended problem, but instead should think about what would nudge the situation in the right direction. Teams discuss their work in progress weekly, either in a brief critique session with me or in a presentation to the whole class, and get feedback. One of my primary tasks as instructor and coach is to help students shape their project into something they can complete in a matter of a few weeks. Usually this means finding a way to focus, reducing the complexity of the project by refining the problem definition and/or the goal. Third, the teams have weekly deadlines over the course of the project to prevent procrastination and help them maintain direction. Fourth, in my critiques of work in progress I may emphasize the most promising or salient elements of their project work and suggest that they prune their project in order to focus on those elements. In this way I am marking critical features of the work. Fellow students may also perform this function during work-in-progress presentations to the class. This part of the work also involves negotiating with students the meaning of their project and its elements.[58]

Frustration control is not usually much of an issue—perhaps students deal with it out of my earshot, or perhaps the engaging quality of the task keeps them forging ahead. Also, I describe wrong turns as part of the design process. Mistakes can be corrected and sometimes can even be generative. A low level of frustration can even help propel breakthroughs. Finally, demonstration as a tutoring function shows up in many ways in the class. We study examples of innovations that have improved particular social, environmental, and economic situations. I also show students a few examples of student work from previous semesters. And the students see the work-in-progress of other teams and learn from those examples and from the feedback that I and others give to those teams.

Design and Problem-Solving Collaboration

External spatial representations aid individual thinking, as we saw in an earlier part of this chapter, but they also play an important role in the work of groups. While these representations are being created, manipulated, and revised by the work of the group, they serve as a referent in the design process, as a record of agreement and as a site for dispute. They emphasize what matters and downplay what is not salient. They serve as a point of reference for group members whose mental models of the task or the object may be quite different, but who can share an artifact that affords pointing and annotation.[59] In the words of Sherry Turkle "When we focus on objects, physicians and philosophers, psychologists and designers, artists and engineers are able to find common ground in everyday experience."[60]

A very basic yet vital example is the "rock drill" that soldiers may perform in the field as they plan their next operation. Standing in a circle, they place rocks on the ground to represent the most important people, equipment, and environmental features of the area they are planning to enter, and move these rocks around as they discuss their anticipated movements and contingency plans. The rocks bear no actual resemblance to the people and things they symbolize, but even in their symbolic form they facilitate group understanding and discussion of the plan of action. Individuals with different roles can point to and move the rocks to illustrate a proposed plan, and the materials are ready to hand in almost any environment.

In an everyday context, an accessible example of an external representation that can take many forms depending on the objectives of the group is the map. A group of students on an Outing Club hike may carry and refer to a topographic map as they follow the trail and calculate the steepness of the terrain and the distance they want to travel. Yet on their drive from the campus to the trailhead they will likely choose a standard road map, which highlights roads and highways but is silent about the contours of the terrain. Stopping in an unfamiliar town after their hike they may consult a tourist map, which exaggerates tourist attractions and local businesses at the expense of other features. In none of these cases is the map a slavish reproduction of the territory. In fact, the usefulness of these maps comes from the fact that they exaggerate some features and omit others. Satellite photos of the terrain are, for some purposes, the most useful, but for these students, as their purposes shift during their outing, satellite photos would be less helpful to their collaborative planning than these other representations.

Maps can also be of key importance to those in professional settings: first responders and hazmat crews, transportation planners, delivery services, geologists and oceanographers, political redistricters, water resource managers, meteorologists—the list is nearly endless. Geographic Information Systems now allow teams the ability to superimpose several types of maps. If a hazmat crew responds to a freight train derailment, they need topographic information (where are the spilled chemicals likely to go as they run downhill?), road maps (what is the best route to the derailment site, on both sides of the tracks?), residential and zoning maps (what types of land use are present near the site, and where might people be living and working?), weather data (if dangerous fumes are released, where will prevailing winds send them?), and other information. These representations are crucial supports for the team of first responders as they plan and execute their response.

In their wide-ranging and insightful study of creative work, Robert and Michele Root-Bernstein highlight modeling as an important thinking tool and point out the enormous variety of possible models in the arts and sciences. A model

> may be a *representational or physical* model, displaying the physical characteristics of a real object; a *functional* model, capturing the essential operations of an object or mechanism; a *theoretical* model, embodying the basic concepts governing the operation of some process; or an *imaginary* model, invented to display the features of something we can't observe directly. . . . All models are distillations of the elements considered to be the most critical determinants of structure and function. They always embody both abstractions and analogies and, usually, dimensional alterations.[61]

At a systems level, collaborators also use objects to think with. Anthropologist Susan Leigh Star coined the term "boundary object" to refer to tools and systems that support collaboration within organizations and among distributed groups of colleagues. She started with a puzzle: how do scientists, who "cooperate without having good models of each other's work . . . employing different units of analysis, methods of aggregating data, and different abstractions of data . . . and with different goals, time horizons, and audiences to satisfy" manage to work productively across all these divisions?[62] A boundary object can be a repository (an archive or museum, for example), an ideal type (a road map, or an atlas of the brain, which is vague enough to support multiple interpretations and purposes, but that nonetheless structures the conversation), a terrain (the boundaries of a state, which can be studied differently by hydrologists, geologists, biologists, and sociologists, all with a shared geographic reference), and labels (shared terminology across groups: "reptile," "granite," "watershed.") An organization or community may employ multiple boundary objects in the course of their work. Boundary objects can also be digital, and increasingly they are. Microsoft Office, Google Docs, the learning management system Blackboard, and major information systems supporting large corporations and governments all have in common the fact that they both support and structure work. In the process they create archives, stimulate the formation of mental models in their users, and use standardized terminology, among many other functions. When they become large, complex, and pervasive enough they even qualify as "boundary infrastructures."[63]

Notes

1. Day, C. L. (1950). Knots and knot lore. *Western Folklore, 9*(3), 229–256.
2. Day, C. L. (1950). Knots and knot lore. *Western Folklore, 9*(3), 229–256.
3. Day, C. L. (1950). Knots and knot lore. *Western Folklore, 9*(3), 229–256.
4. Reefe, T. Q. (1977). Lukasa: A Luba memory device. *African Arts, 10*(4), 49–50.
5. Reefe, T. Q. (1977). Lukasa: A Luba memory device. *African Arts, 10*(4), 49–50.
6. Yates, F. A. (1966). *The art of memory*. Chicago, IL: The University of Chicago Press.
7. Foer, J. (2012). *Moonwalking with Einstein: The art and science of remembering everything*. New York, NY: Penguin.
8. Zielinski, S. (2014, February 3) The secrets of Sherlock's mind palace. *Smithsonian Magazine*. Retrieved from www.smithsonianmag.com/arts-culture/secrets-sherlocks-mind-palace-180949567/.
9. Willard, E. (1849). *Willard's historic guide: Guide to the temple of time, and universal history for schools*. New York, NY: A. S. Barnes & Company. Retrieved from https://lccn.loc.gov/03006044
10. Willard, E. (1846). *Standing within the temple of time [Printed chart]*. New York, NY: A. S. Barnes & Co. Retrieved from https://blogs.princeton.edu/rarebooks/2008/12/standing-within-the-temple-of/comment-page-1/.

11. Costa, A. J., Silva, J. B. L., Chagas, P. P., Krinzinger, H., Lonneman, J., Willmes, K., . . . Haase, V. G. (2011). A hand full of numbers: A role for offloading in arithmetics learning? *Frontiers in Psychology, 2*, 1–16.
12. Kim, M. J., & Maher, M. L. (2008). The impact of tangible user interfaces on spatial cognition during collaborative design. *Design Studies, 29*(3), 222–253.
13. Kuhn, S., & Davidson, J. (2007). Thinking with things, teaching with things: Enhancing student learning in qualitative research through reflective use of tools and materials. *Qualitative Research Journal*, 7(2), 63–75.
14. Miller, G. A. (1956). The magical number seven, plus or minus two: Some limits on our capacity for processing information. *Psychological Review, 63*(2), 81–97.
15. Gobet, F., Lane, P. C., Croker, S., Cheng, P. C., Jones, G., Oliver, I., & Pine, J. M. (2001). Chunking mechanisms in human learning. *Trends in Cognitive Sciences, 5*(6), 236–243.
16. Rosenberg, S. (2008). *Dreaming in code: Two dozen programmers, three years, 4,732 bugs, and one quest for transcendent software*. New York, NY: Three Rivers Press.
17. Brown, P. C., Roediger, H. L., & McDaniel, M. A. (2014). *Make it stick*. Cambridge, MA: Harvard University Press.
18. National Research Council, & Geographical Sciences Committee. (2005). *Learning to think spatially*. Washington, DC: National Academies Press.
19. Hein, G. E. (1966). Kekule and the architecture of molecules. *Advances in Chemistry, 61*, 1–12.
20. Vinten-Johansen, P., Brody, H., Paneth, N., Rachman, S., Rip, M., & Zuck, D. (2003). *Cholera, chloroform, and the science of medicine: A life of John Snow*. New York, NY: Oxford University Press.
21. Root-Bernstein, R., & Root-Bernstein, M. (1999). *Sparks of genius: The thirteen thinking tools of the world's most creative people* (p. 220). Boston, MA: Houghton Mifflin.
22. Root-Bernstein, R., & Root-Bernstein, M. (1999). *Sparks of genius: The thirteen thinking tools of the world's most creative people* (p. 219). Boston, MA: Houghton Mifflin.
23. National Research Council, & Geographical Sciences Committee. (2005). *Learning to think spatially*. Washington, DC: National Academies Press.
24. National Research Council, & Geographical Sciences Committee. (2005). *Learning to think spatially* (p. 3). Washington, DC: National Academies Press.
25. Craft, A. (2005). *Creativity in schools: Tensions and dilemmas* (p. 36). New York, NY: Routledge.
26. Bamberger, J., & Schön, D. A. (1983). Learning as reflective conversation with materials: Notes from work in progress. *Art Education, 36*(2), 68–73. p. 68.
27. Bamberger, J., & Schön, D. A. (1983). Learning as reflective conversation with materials: Notes from work in progress. *Art Education, 36*(2), 68–73. p. 69.
28. Bamberger, J., & Schön, D. A. (1983). Learning as reflective conversation with materials: Notes from work in progress. *Art Education, 36*(2), 68–73. pp. 69–70 and 73. Emphasis in the original.
29. Itten, J. (1975). *Design and form: The basic course at the Bauhaus and later* (p. 7). Hoboken, NJ: Wiley & Sons.
30. Gibson, J. J. (1977). The theory of affordances. In R. Shaw & J. Bransford (Eds.), *Perceiving, acting, and knowing: Toward an ecological psychology* (pp. 67–82). Hillsdale, NJ: Lawrence Erlbaum.
31. Stravinsky, I. (1970). *Poetics of music in the form of six lessons* (Vol. 66). Cambridge, MA: Harvard University Press. p. 65.
32. Demetrios, E. (2001). *An Eames primer* (p. 168). New York, NY: Universe Publishing.
33. Rosenberg, S. (2008). *Dreaming in code: Two dozen programmers, three years, 4,732 bugs, and one quest for transcendent software* (p. 261). New York, NY: Three Rivers Press.
34. Turkle, S. (2007). *Evocative objects: Things we think with* (p. 5). Cambridge, MA: The MIT Press.

35. Turkle, S. (2007). *Evocative objects: Things we think with* (p. 314). Cambridge, MA: The MIT Press.
36. Johnson, M. (2007). *The meaning of the body: Aesthetics of human understanding* (pp. ix, xi). Chicago, IL: The University of Chicago Press.
37. Lakoff, G., & Johnson, M. (1980). *Metaphors we live by*. Chicago, IL: The University of Chicago Press.
38. Arnheim, R. (1969). *Visual thinking* (p. 118). Berkeley, CA: University of California Press.
39. Lakoff, G., & Johnson, M. (1980). *Metaphors we live by* (p. 5). Chicago, IL: The University of Chicago Press.
40. Schön, D. A. (1993). Generative metaphor: A perspective on problem-setting in social policy. In A. Ortony (Ed.), *Metaphor and thought* (2nd ed., p. 140). Cambridge, UK: Cambridge University Press.
41. Menand, L. (2010). *The marketplace of ideas*. New York, NY: W. W. Norton & Company.
42. Papert, S. (1991). Situating Constructionism. In S. Papert & I. Harel (Eds.), *Constructionism: Research reports and essays, 1985–1990* (p. 1). Santa Barbara, CA: Praeger.
43. Arnheim, R. (1969). *Visual thinking* (pp. 296–297). Berkeley, CA: University of California Press.
44. Isaacson, W. (2007). *Einstein: His life and universe*. New York, NY: Simon & Schuster Paperbacks.
45. Keller, E. F. (1984). *A feeling for the organism, 10th anniversary edition: The life and work of Barbara McClintock*. New York, NY: Henry Holt & Company.
46. Keller, E. F. (1984). *A feeling for the organism, 10th anniversary edition: The life and work of Barbara McClintock* (p. 117). New York, NY: Henry Holt & Company.
47. Keller, E. F. (1984). *A feeling for the organism, 10th anniversary edition: The life and work of Barbara McClintock*. New York, NY: Henry Holt & Company.
48. Root-Bernstein, R., & Root-Bernstein, M. (1999). *Sparks of genius: The thirteen thinking tools of the world's most creative people* (p. 196). Boston, MA: Houghton Mifflin.
49. Abbott, E. A. (1894/1952). *Flatland: A romance of many dimensions*. New York, NY: Dover Publications.
50. Papert, S. (1980). *Mindstorms: Children, computers, and powerful ideas* (p. 63). New York, NY: Basic Books.
51. Damasio, A. (1999). *The feeling of what happens: Body and emotion in the making of consciousness*. San Diego, CA: Harcourt.
52. Wood, D., Bruner, J. S., & Ross, G. (1976). The role of tutoring in problem solving. *Journal of Child Psychology and Psychiatry, 17*(2), 89–100.
53. Wood, D., Bruner, J. S., & Ross, G. (1976). The role of tutoring in problem solving. *Journal of Child Psychology and Psychiatry, 17*(2), 89–100. p. 98.
54. Vygotsky, L. S. (1978). *Mind in society: The development of higher psychological processes*. Cambridge, MA: Harvard University Press.
55. Dewey, J. (1938/1997). *Experience and education* (p. 75). New York, NY: Touchstone.
56. Wilson, F. (1998). *The hand: How its use shapes the brain, language, and human culture* (p. 254). New York, NY: Vintage Books.
57. Lakoff, G., & Nunez, R. (2000). *Where mathematics comes from: How the embodied mind brings mathematics into being*. New York, NY: Basic Books.
58. East, K. (2009). Content: Making IT a boundary object in the college classroom. *College Teaching, 57*(2), 119–125.
59. National Research Council, & Geographical Sciences Committee. (2005). *Learning to think spatially*. Washington, DC: National Academies Press.

60. Turkle, S. (2007). *Evocative objects: Things we think with* (p. 8). Cambridge, MA: The MIT Press.
61. Root-Bernstein, R., & Root-Bernstein, M. (1999). *Sparks of genius: The thirteen thinking tools of the world's most creative people* (p. 229). Boston, MA: Houghton Mifflin.
62. Star, S. L. (1998). The structure of ill-structured solutions: Boundary objects and heterogeneous distributed problem solving. *Distributed Artificial Intelligence, 2*, 37–54. p. 46.
63. Bowker, G. C., & Star, S. L. (2000). *Sorting things out: Classification and its consequences.* Cambridge, MA: The MIT Press.

Interlude D: Qualitative Research Software

In this book, my focus has been on tangible things to think with, inhabiting space in the physical world. This is not to deny that digital things can be rich tools and provocations for deep thinking. My choice to focus on the non-digital world stems largely from the fact that, in education in the last generation or so, I feel we have leapfrogged over the physical and the analog and focused almost exclusively on the digital, to the detriment of the embodied learners we are trying to teach. Still, I don't want the digital world to be entirely absent from this book.

Perhaps the most famous example in education of a fruitful digital thing to think with is Seymour Papert's Logo. Logo is a simple, child-friendly programming language which in its early incarnations was paired with a robotic "turtle" that could be commanded by children by way of the computer-based instructions they wrote. Papert's work (for example his 1980 book *Mindstorms*[1]) has had an enormous impact on the education community, demonstrating how in capable hands the computer can be a site of deep learning, not just training on how to use software and the Internet. Countless educators and innovators have created curricula and new digital systems, like the products Lego Mindstorms and Scratch visual programming, inspired by Papert's insights.

A quite different example from the world of higher education is my and my colleagues' experience with software called "NVivo." NVivo is a tool used by scholars who are conducting qualitative research—that is, who are working with non-numerical data such as interview transcripts, memoranda, reports, and images. The academy has long used computers to analyze numerical data and has had associated software tools to conduct statistical analyses on numerical data sets large and small. Qualitative research, on the other hand, has until recently been conducted using paper records. A qualitative researcher, even a doctoral student, might have paper records filling multiple file cabinets, with interview transcripts, field notes, documents from the community being studied, paper forms demonstrating the informed consent of the human subjects who participated in the study, and so on. When the researcher starts to code these documents (by highlighting passages that are associated with particular topics), the amount of paper proliferates further. And as part of the analysis of the data, the documents were often cut up and sorted by the code with which they were associated, in order to begin to see patterns in the data, a key step in analysis.

With NVivo and other qualitative research software, all this work is performed on digital documents. Suddenly, student work can be carried on a memory stick or posted to a class web site. In the days of paper, professors and fellow students would be unlikely to look through drawers of filing cabinets to see the raw material of a student's project; now that material can

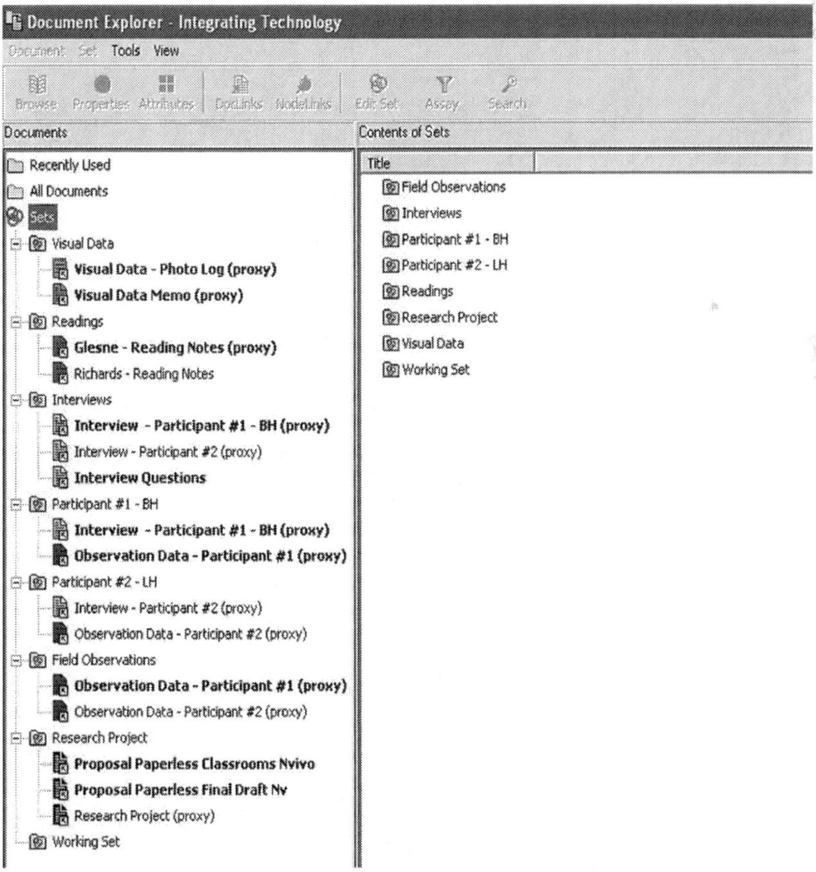

Figure D.1 One of many ways of viewing a project using NVivo qualitative research software.

be visible and easily explored. Students can get more relevant and thorough feedback from their peers and their instructors, and can use the software to explore questions about their data easily and in real time.

My colleague Judy Davidson put the use of NVivo at the center of her doctoral-level qualitative research methods course. Not only did her students need to learn and use the tool, but NVivo was also the vehicle for their in-class presentations of their work. Davidson calls the new format the "electronic project (qualitative research project materials stored and manipulated electronically)"[2] and found that the use of electronic projects transformed her classes.

In addition to portability and transparency, this digital tool allows students to see their project in multiple and novel ways. As they gain experience with qualitative research and with NVivo, students develop an ability to do what Davidson calls "reading the project."[3] Students learn through working with their own data and by observing other students' class presentations how to identify and interpret important patterns in their data. They learn to use NVivo's powerful tools, such as search functions and modeling tools that can create graphic representations of their project. Davidson considers this a form of literacy, and like literacy, a student's facility with NVivo allows them to see information represented in a new medium.

A key characteristic of a thinking-with-things approach is that it can present students with distinct representations in a variety of media, strengthening learning and promoting understanding. NVivo effectively supports a variety of representations and allows students to move between representations quickly and with minimal effort. Instead of wading through file drawers full of documents, a student researcher can quickly pose "what if" questions and explore alternative ways of framing both research questions and research results. Far more than a simple bookkeeping tool, qualitative research software is a thing to think with.

Notes

1. Papert, S. (1980). *Mindstorms: Children, computers, and powerful ideas.* New York, NY: Basic Books.
2. Kuhn, S., & Davidson, J. (2007). Thinking with things, teaching with things: Enhancing student learning in qualitative research through reflective use of tools and materials. *Qualitative Research Journal,* 7(2), 63–75.
3. Davidson, J. (2005). *Learning to 'read' NVivo projects: Implications for teaching qualitative research.* Paper presented at the 2nd Teaching Qualitative Research Using QSR Products Conference, University of Wisconsin, Madison, WI.

Abstraction Reconsidered 5

Given all the benefits of thinking with things, why don't we do more of it in the classroom? What is holding us back? In this chapter, I focus on one particular barrier to better teaching practice: the timeworn distinction between the "abstract" and the "concrete." Although rarely discussed and never well defined in the academy, the concrete has about it the whiff of the simple, the primitive, the specific, the particular and therefore the provincial. Abstraction, on the other hand, is the general, the transcendent, the essential, the ultimate goal of the life of the mind. The modern university, venerating abstraction, has an uneasy relationship with the concrete, especially with the tangible. Of course, we must have science labs and art studios, but in general, learning spaces where students interact with physical objects are few. The vacuous classrooms of which I have complained are generally considered perfect for the primary work of the university, which is the examination and transmission of abstractions. Because we are innocent of any notion that cognition is embodied, or that thought and learning are interactive activities, we may even see our sensory deprivation chambers as beneficial to learning because they lack distractions. This is a key obstacle to an improved pedagogy which will allow students to think with things.

The tension between the abstract, immaterial, conceptual, and ideal on the one hand and the concrete, specific, tangible, situated, and embodied on the other hand has a millennia-long history which I only allude to here and there over the course of this book, but the evidence suggests that for much of recorded history there has been something resembling the distinction between the abstract and the concrete, and that where that distinction existed there has generally been a higher value placed on one or on the other. Sometimes the value distinction weighs in favor of the concrete, but often it is in favor of the abstract as the superior form of knowledge and of learning. I have already quoted William James on the Greeks; here I will mention the way in which a passage from the extraordinarily influential 17th-century English Philosopher John Locke reveals (and gently challenges) the values of his age. Like many Enlightenment figures, he had an interest in education, and late in life published *Some Thoughts Concerning Education*, a treatise on the education of gentlemen in class-bound England. Toward the end of the *Thoughts*, Locke anticipates the reaction of his readers' prejudices:

> I have one more thing to add, which as soon as I mention, I shall run the danger of being suspected to have forgot what I am about, and what I have above written concerning education, all tending towards a gentleman's calling, with which a trade seems wholly to be inconsistent. And yet, I cannot forbear to say, I would have him [the gentleman-in-training] learn a trade, a manual trade; nay, two or three, but one more particularly.[1]

The prejudice against trades continues in many quarters in higher education in 20th-century America, and it takes a number of forms, including the sometimes-uneasy place of professional education and of explicit career preparation in the academy. I see it, too, among some of my colleagues in the humanities and social sciences, as well as some in the sciences and engineering. In teaching social science, I often use physical materials in classroom exercises, and in past years I frequently taught classes in locations where other faculty would walk past my classroom. Some colleagues gave me strange looks when they saw my students building with Lego, making Tinkertoy concept maps, or creating autobiographical collages about their research interests. Perhaps it is the happy chatter coming from my classroom as students build that first attracts their attention. One colleague stuck his head in and said, as if in jest, "you're having too much fun." A student I had just recruited as a graduate assistant told me that one humanities professor had warned her about me, and described her work with me with the derogatory "playing with Lego." I hasten to add that many colleagues have embraced the idea of thinking with things in the classroom and are eager to understand how to put into practice their intuitive sense that this approach has value.

The distinction between the concrete and the abstract is important to examine because, like the mind/body distinction and other ideas, I've come to believe that it lurks behind many of our assumptions and practices in higher education. When we use these words, we assume that we know what they mean and what their implications are for learning; but in fact, when we look under the rug, we find that this distinction is far more problematic than we take it to be. As Rudolf Arnheim says,

> The misleading dichotomy between perceiving and thinking is reflected in the practice of distinguishing 'abstract' from 'concrete' things as though they belonged to two mutually exclusive sets. . . . It is equally misleading to call concrete that which is physical and abstract that which is mental.[2]

It is difficult to let go of the terms "concrete" and "abstract," just as it is to let go of "mind" and "body," because we don't have more nuanced replacements, but it is important as we use them to keep in mind how problematic they are.

Piaget's Stage Theory

There is an important 20th-century source of confusion about the abstract/concrete distinction and its implications for education. The eminent scholar of child development and pioneer in laboratory studies of children's cognition, Jean Piaget, is rightly celebrated in educational circles for his more than half-century of close study of the nature and development of children's knowledge. A discussion of Piaget's work, particularly his stage theory of development, appears in almost all textbooks on education and on introductory psychology. Even when Piaget and his work are not mentioned explicitly, it has become an article of faith that, for example, children below the age of 7 are unable to perform certain sorts of mental operations, and that good pedagogy should be tailored to the child's stage of development (and therefore, generally, the child's age).

Piaget posited four stages of child and adolescent development. Each stage has several sub-stages, and Piaget admitted the possibility that there could also be additional major stages later in development.[3]

- The first stage, the sensorimotor period, begins at birth. It lasts about two years, during which time the infant begins to organize and coordinate its actions and perceptions. Actions that begin as reflexes, such as sucking and grasping, develop to become voluntary. Babies learn to coordinate vision and touch, and to repeat actions that have positive or pleasurable outcomes. They experiment with objects, learning that they are permanent, and try new behaviors.
- At around age 2, the preoperational period begins. The child begins to use language and to engage in pretend play, such as when a broom can be ridden like a horse, and pillows can be arranged to build a fort.

Children engage in social play, although they have difficulty imagining a point of view other than their own. Later in this stage, children are starting to reason about logic and causality but do not fully grasp some basic concepts. This is the period of the perpetual "Why?"
- The concrete operations stage begins around age 6 or 7. Children begin to develop logical structures for hierarchical categories applying to actual objects or events, although not to generalizations. Children are often able to put things in order, perform some mathematical operations on numbers, and reason with some categories (my pet is a parakeet, a parakeet is a kind of bird, etc.).
- Beginning around age 11 or 12, children enter the formal operations stage. They begin to be able to form hypotheses and reason about categories and immaterial objects and concepts. They develop the ability to, for example, design simple scientific experiments to test propositions, and image possible results of the testing. They become able to solve problems methodically rather than through trial and error, and begin to be able to observe and reason about their own reasoning processes (metacognition). They are more able to see that others may have a different point of view, and to reason about values and life choices.

In a famous experiment illustrating the difference between children's pre-operational and concrete operational thinking, a child is presented with two water glasses, one short and fat and the other tall and thin. A quantity of water is in one glass; then, as the child watches, the water is poured from one glass to the other. A pre-operational child, asked whether one glass contains more water than the other, will say that the taller glass has more water. As my description indicates, both glasses, when full, have the same amount of water, but the preoperational child only attends to the height of the water, and sees a higher water level in the tall, thin glass. For us adults, this is an extraordinary result, because we have the concept of "conservation" and know that the amount of water remains constant as it is poured from one glass to the other, but the preoperational child does not. Another experiment, demonstrating the same lack of conservation in children under seven, involves taking a number of coins, say five, and laying them in a row in front of the child. With the child watching, you can make the row shorter by decreasing the space between the coins, or make the row longer by increasing, without changing the number of coins. A preoperational child will say there are more coins when the row is longer. (I urge you to find a 5- or 6-year-old and try this yourself. If you don't have a child handy, there are videos on the Internet. But it's much more fun with a real child.)

For our purposes, the timing and content of the *formal operations* stage is the most important. If college students are abstract thinkers, it is because they have reached the stage of formal operations. It has become, however, conventional wisdom to read Piaget's work to mean that, after about age 12—and certainly by age 18 when students typically enter college—young people are able to think in and deal with abstractions in general. Surely college students are capable of many abstractions of the sort that Piaget believed learners in the formal operations stage come to master, but it does not follow that they are adept at handling all or most formalisms, particularly those that are new to them. In his later work, Piaget acknowledged that the ability to use formal operations in one domain did not necessarily mean that the learner could use it in all domains. According to Campbell,

> Textbooks nearly always say that formal operations are universal—that is, every normal person acquires them. . . . Piaget used to believe [this] claim, but abandoned it in the early 1970s, when he was faced with evidence that a substantial percentage of college freshmen cannot design and carry out a good pendulum experiment or rod-bending experiment.[4]

Stage theories in general, particularly when applied to a phenomenon as complex as human development, are prone to being oversimplified when they are interpreted and applied. This is true even when the original theory is nuanced and evolving, as is the case with Piaget's stages. Yet the "textbook version" of Piaget's theory, as Campbell points out, has been streamlined and simplified, sometimes to the point that developmental stages come to resemble the stages of a rocket, in which each stage in turn provides the motive energy, then is discarded, giving way to a new stage, which then in turn falls away, and so forth. This is emphatically not the way in which developmental stages work in human beings. Instead, if you want a simple metaphor, the relationship of the foundation of a house (which comes first, and is usually quite simple and solid—the alternate meaning of the word concrete!) is more apt. You can't have a house without a foundation, and the foundation remains key, even as the rest of the house is built and inhabited. The foundation is the "ground truth" on which the house rests.

To illustrate some of the complexity that must be present in a stage theory if it is to be at all accurate, consider an extended theoretical analysis by developmental psychologist John H. Flavell.[5] He identifies five different principal ways in which a cognitive "item" (a skill, behavior, etc., which he calls X_1.) can be said to be related to a later-developing cognitive item X_2 The five types of relationships are:

- *Addition*, in which a new skill is added to a cognitive repertoire in the way in which one would add a screwdriver to a toolbox that already has a hammer.
- *Substitution*, in which a new skill or behavior fully replaces an earlier one, as one would learn to see a short, fat glass as having the same amount of water even though the water came from a tall glass.
- *Modification*, as when an existing skill, like hammering, becomes differentiated, so that in some situations a very light tap with a pencil might be used, and in other situations a heavy hit with a mallet.
- *Inclusion*, in which an earlier-developing cognitive item is integrated into a later developing skill, as when a child learns to understand a ratio because the (earlier developing) ability to hold two things in mind at once has been subsumed into the later developing item.
- *Mediation*, in which an earlier developing item is an indispensable prerequisite for a later developing item, but is not included in it, as with an infant's pushing, which contributes to the development of a notion of objects which are separate from the infant—but once the idea of external objects is developed, they need not necessarily be pushed to be perceived.

As Flavell also points out, each of these types has a number of sub-types, and when one adds in the problem of how to verify these relationships experimentally, one reaches a startling level of complexity. As Flavell laments,

> the categories finally arrived at have simply not proven to be the unitary, nonoverlapping, definitionally elegant affairs originally hoped for. As will become apparent, cognitive-developmental sequences appear to resist vigorously being sorted into neat, mutually exclusive, logical groupings. Each increment of neatness and consistency imported into any classification system here always seems to be paid for with a loss of classificatory fit across the range of concrete cases it was intended to describe.[6]

That is not to say that there are no cognitive-developmental sequences, or that humans develop at random. Clearly some aspects of development are precursors to others—many of the milestones of the preoperational stage depend on capabilities developed during the sensorimotor stage, and concrete operations are not possible without the elements of the pre-operational stage. Still, the notion of developmental sequences is highly complex and full of contingencies, and we should certainly not presume particular capacities in our college freshmen simply because they come to us in late adolescence. Flavell concludes that in educational settings, "this sort of [learning] process—tortuous and spiral-like, cyclical and recursive, sequence-violating and sequence-transforming—may be characteristic of most cognitive activity and development."[7]

Teaching Abstraction

In the face of this complexity, we need a more appropriate and nuanced approach to instruction. Our goal of guiding students toward greater levels of facility with formalism and abstract thinking is still a worthy one, but our tactics must change. So often in college, formalisms are conveyed in lectures and textbooks—that is, in passive rather than active formats, conducive to memorization rather than to inquiry. Students are expected to digest and recall propositions without understanding how these conclusions were arrived at, let alone have the opportunity to explore and manipulate, drawing their own conclusions. Uri Wilensky, writing about university level mathematics instruction, says it is too often a

> "litany" of definition/proof/theorem chanted day in and day out. . . . This image of mathematics practice portrays mathematics as a dead subject—inquiry is unnecessary because our concepts have been formally defined in the "right" way . . . using linear deductive style, stipulative definitions, and non-contextual proofs. Very little effort is put into motivating the mathematical ideas, linking them to other ideas both mathematical and non-mathematical, or any discussion of the "meaning" of the mathematics being taught.[8]

In these situations, students often resort, as I did in my own math education, to simply implementing rote procedures, without understanding the underlying concepts or building new intuitions about the phenomena they are studying. In many cases, students can get very good grades in classes without having any meaningful understanding of the ideas underlying the procedures they are implementing. Wilensky describes a case in which some new probability and statistics software, designed for use by students taking college level statistics courses, was used by large numbers of students in many different statistics classes. Although they had spent hours and hours plotting random variables, almost none of them could give a really satisfactory answer to one of the questions on the final test, "What is a random variable?"[9] The inability to understand or explain very basic concepts in statistics is the rule, rather than the exception, for scholars who have passed university level statistics courses, at least among Wilensky's sample, which included advanced doctoral students and even PhDs.

The inability of students to connect classroom formalisms to embodied experience has deep and lasting consequences. Knowledge that is unconnected to the embodied knower is brittle and difficult to apply. A gifted undergraduate physics student might ace the exam on torque, but not understand that it means that a heavy door is most easily opened by pushing on the edge furthest from the hinge.[10] As Henri Poincaré said of secondary school graduates in France, "For them the world of science and that of reality are shut off in water-tight compartments."[11]

"Abstraction is a great tool for the furtherance of human inquiry," says Mark Johnson, but when taken to an extreme and disconnected from our embodied understanding, "it is also responsible for much of the loss of meaning that is available to us in any given situation."[12] A similar sentiment was expressed by economist Robert Heilbroner, who said more than once that "the prestige accorded to mathematics in economics has given it rigor, but, alas, also mortis."[13]

Productive abstraction is always, implicitly or explicitly, grounded in concrete embodied experience. In fact, the act of forming and manipulating abstractions is always in conversation with the specific and the embodied. Rudolf Arnheim describes one of the ways in which, in everyday action, the abstract and the concrete are intertwined.

> When a college student is asked to copy what he sees under the microscope, he cannot aim, mechanically, for mere accuracy and neatness. He must decide what matters and what types of relevant shapes are represented in the accidental specimen. Therefore, his drawing cannot possibly be a reproduction; it will be an image of what he sees and understands, more or less actively and intelligently.[14]

The student is abstracting, "drawing out" (to use the Latin root of the word), actively extracting from the unique complexity of a particular situation the features he sees as key. He is constructing his understanding, which may then be critiqued by his professor. Her feedback will shape what he sees the next time he looks through the microscope. In this way, professional vision is developed. Expanding on this point, Arnheim says,

> The experienced physician, mechanic, or physiologist looking at a wound, an engine, a microscopic preparation, "sees" things that the novice does not see. If both, experts and laymen, were asked to make exact copies of what they see, their drawings would be quite different.[15]

Interestingly, a physical model—as used in engineering, chemistry, and many other fields—is also an abstraction in that it emphasizes particular features and hides or downplays others that are not salient for the user's purposes. A physical model, then, is an abstraction, but also "concrete" in the sense of being specific and tangible. Further proof that we are not dealing with neat categories here!

Perhaps it is the very fact that physical models straddle the worlds of the concrete, specific, "found object" and that of the mental Platonic ideal that makes them productive things to think with. In what ways is this model like, and unlike, the thing of which it is a model? What can we learn from these similarities and differences? As embodied learners, we feel our way into abstractions, and when we have representations that help us along the path we can develop a much firmer grasp on ideas, generalities, categories. Productive work with abstractions stands on the shoulders of sensory experience, as a house stands on its foundation.

Perhaps the most celebrated public monument to the value of physical models in science learning is the Exploratorium, the San Francisco museum dedicated to hands-on science discovery. The brainchild of Frank Oppenheimer, a distinguished 20th-century physicist and younger brother of J. Robert Oppenheimer, the Exploratorium has as perhaps its most central principle the idea that the best science learning grows from personal, physical interaction with brilliantly designed exhibits that can be hit, adjusted, aimed, and so forth, and that through sustained personal interaction a visitor can make interesting and informative observations about important phenomena in physics. These ideas were in Frank even before he founded the Exploratorium. Like his brother Robert before him, he built with blocks, and attended New York's Ethical Culture school, where block play and Froebel training still held sway. As a professor of physics at the University of Colorado, as he was gradually emerging from the devastation of being blacklisted during the McCarthy era, Oppenheimer created what he called a "library of experiments."[16] With colleagues, he created a series of carts that students could borrow and use. Each cart held the apparatus for a physical experiment designed to accompany the material of lower-division classes in physics. With at least 65 carts available, students had extensive opportunity to interact with physical apparatus that facilitated the exploration of principles in physics.

During this time, Oppenheimer began to dream about a hands-on science museum. In his first public statement about the project that led to the creation of the Exploratorium, he wrote about the shortcomings of science education conducted through television, magazines, books, and introductory science courses.

> But such attempts, although valuable, are at a disadvantage because they lack props; they require apparatus which people can see and handle and which display phenomena which people can turn on and off and vary at will. Explaining science and technology without props can resemble an attempt to tell what it is like to swim without ever letting a person near the water.[17]

Although Oppenheimer's position remains a minority opinion, the longevity, popularity, and frequent attempts at imitation of the Exploratorium speak to the power of this conviction and the way in which it resonates with science educators and with the public. In place of the usual textbook-based teaching, in which abstractions developed by experts are transmitted to students without allowing the students to construct their own knowledge, Exploratorium visitors have a personal encounter with selected phenomena in the physical world, carefully curated by museum staff. Now that we know that knowing and learning are embodied, faculty not only in physics but across the disciplines can draw inspiration from the Exploratorium.

One of the most interesting and, to my mind, productive challenges to the idea that the job of the university is to teach abstractions comes from the notion that abstraction can be equated with "distance from the self." This phenomenological perspective has important implications. More than 50 years ago, Merleau-Ponty, in *The Phenomenology of Perception*, said,

> For each object . . . there is an optimum distance from which it requires to be seen . . . a living body, seen at too close quarters, and divorced from any background against which it can stand out, is no longer a living body but a mass of matter as outlandish as a lunar landscape. . . . Again, seen from too great a distance, the body loses its living value, and is seen simply as a puppet or automation.[18]

Scale, and with it a sense of embodied orientation to the phenomenon, is key to our ability to grasp a concept. I recall extended conversations with psychologist Emlee Kohler, who was struggling to teach her students about the structure and function of the neuron. We met at a Lego workshop for faculty I was leading, and Kohler's intuition was that allowing students to construct physical models of the neuron with Lego might help their learning. "The neuron is abstract because of its size," she told me. A model at human scale, she thought, would bring the neuron into focus, following Merleau-Ponty, and allow students a firmer understanding of important aspects of its structure. She later reported to me that adding a study session in which students built models of the neuron with Lego led to a significant improvement in their test scores.

Interestingly, "distance from the self" seems not only to challenge cognition, but also moral and emotional judgement. Psychologist and behavioral economist Dan Ariely and his students surveyed 12,000 US golfers about whether they thought the average golfer would cheat at golf in any of three ways: by moving the ball four inches to a new and more favorable position with their hand, with their shoe, or with a tap from a club. Confirming previous experiments in other domains, Ariely and his collaborators found that those surveyed were more likely to say that a golfer would move the ball with a club—the most distant from the self, because mediated by a tool—and least likely to move it with the hand. "Dishonesty in golf, much as in our other experiments, is indeed directly influenced by the psychological distance from the action. Cheating becomes much simpler when there are more steps between us and the dishonest act."[19]

In *Connected Mathematics*, Uri Wilensky puts forth a novel and generative reframing of what it is to be "concrete."[20] Heeding the call of Turkle and Papert[21] to "re-value" the concrete in learning environments, Wilensky notes the brittle knowledge of students who learn procedures and formalisms but never really make them their own. They may be able to solve the textbook problems, but they do not have a robust and flexible grasp of the fundamental ideas of the discipline they are studying. For these students, the ideas of mathematics truly are abstractions, in some of the senses found in the Oxford English Dictionary: difficult to understand, abstruse, separate, set apart from, lacking awareness of context.[22]

Reversing the assumption that learning proceeds from the concrete to the abstract, Wilensky argues that objects—physical objects but also, importantly, ideas, concepts, formalisms—*become* concrete for us as our relationship to them becomes richer and more varied.

> The more connections we make between an object and other objects, the more concrete it becomes for us. The richer the set of representations of the object, the more ways we have of interacting with it, the more concrete it is for us. Concreteness, then, is that property which measures the degree of our relatedness to the object (the richness of our representations, interactions, connections with the object), how close we are to it, or, if you will, the *quality of our relationship* with the object.[23]

Wilensky's argument is that, developmentally, all things start as abstractions of a sort, and it is only through exploration and familiarity, through constructing a relationship with an object, a person, or an idea, that a thing becomes concrete. Infants have to develop "object constancy"—the understanding that an object that passes behind a curtain still exists and could reappear, for example. Piaget, and today many if not most educators, see knowledge as constructed by the learner through experience and exploration. In this view, we make a new object or idea concrete for ourselves through interaction, discovery, forming multiple representations, and making connections to other things we already know. This process, which Wilensky calls *concretion*,[24] takes time and effort, but can be helped along by a conducive learning environment, including scaffolding by a sympathetic tutor and appropriate materials. The result is a durable, usable, meaningful relationship with something that began as remote, distant, and detached. Rudolf Arnheim also finds the loss of meaning inherent in our conventional teaching, involving the direct communication of abstractions, disturbing and wrong-headed.

> The teacher is tempted to lose, in the transmission of textbook data, the sense of what these data are about. . . . It is a pathological detachment. But it is equated with the highest form of human intelligence if abstraction is considered a withdrawal from direct experience.[25]

Even expert scholars struggle with the loss of meaning, especially when they have been inculcated with the view that Arnheim is critiquing: that the pinnacle of intelligence is withdrawal, personal removal. Alice Koller, a mid-career philosopher troubled by her professional experience as a knower who felt somewhat estranged from her subject, said "The part of me that never amalgamated with philosophy" was desperately looking for a path to integration.[26] Wilensky's perspective helps to make sense of the seemingly unrelated alternate definition of concrete: a building material that is an amalgam of stone, sand, and cement. To make something concrete is thus to construct, combine, and integrate.

Because "abstraction" has many meanings, it is important that we not lose sight of the valuable ideas to which it points. While the absolute withdrawal from human experience can indeed be pathological and cause loss of meaning, we also use the word abstraction to point to important concepts. Perhaps David Hilbert, one of the foremost mathematicians of the late 19th and early 20th century, can help us:

> In mathematics, as in any scientific research, we find two tendencies present. On the one hand, the tendency toward *abstraction* seeks to crystallize the *logical* relations inherent in the maze of material being studied, and to correlate the material in a systematic and orderly manner. On the other hand, the tendency toward *intuitive understanding* fosters a more immediate grasp of the objects one studies, a live *rapport* with them, so to speak, which stresses the concrete meaning of their relations.[27]

Intuitive understanding in mathematics, as in other fields, is something that develops over time, and is closely linked to concretion. Notice that Hilbert uses words like *grasp* and *rapport*, as well as *concrete*, to describe the experience of mathematical intuition. Yet the logical structure and systematic ordering, which Hilbert calls abstraction, is also essential to success and innovation in mathematics and across the disciplines. Experts have not only extensive factual knowledge, but their knowledge is also well structured.[28] In Piaget's developmental scheme, "formal operations" captures the idea that there is a formal structure to more advanced thought. In academia, there is consensus that developing students' abilities in the domain of formal thought—abstractions—is a central goal of higher education. The question is, how to get there?

The standard answer is direct attack. Formalisms are presented in textbooks, tested in exams, and described in lectures. Instructors assume that students are developmentally ready to tackle abstractions head on. And many are, if they have the prior experience and the intuitions needed to grasp the material and make it their own, building the many connections that lead to deep understanding—to concretion, in Wilensky's terms. But many others struggle, unable to construct the connections and make the meaning they will need if they are to have more than a brittle relationship with what they are given to learn. For them, scaffolding, time to build connections, and things—as Frank Oppenheimer would say, props—are vital to building a connection, Hilbert's *rapport*, with new concepts.

I am put in mind of a senior colleague, in another department, with whom I once taught a graduate seminar. He was a dedicated teacher and a mentor to many graduate students over a long career. He came to our once-a-week three-hour class meeting one day with a PowerPoint presentation that had at least 300 slides. If you have ever sat through a slide presentation—as so many of us have—you know that to teach that much material could take several weeks, even a whole semester. Yet my colleague thought he could march through his slide deck in a single class. His intentions were deeply generous—he wanted to give his students, who were mostly from working class families and sacrificing time and money to attend graduate school—as much value as possible for their money. What he didn't understand, though, is that he needed to give students time to interrogate and play with the ideas he was presenting. A brief exposure to a slide does not translate automatically to learning, and certainly not to anything more than a very superficial understanding of the material. The challenge for instructors is to find the right balance of quantity of material and quality of learning.

As we have already established, earlier concrete, embodied modes of thinking do not disappear as a learner becomes able to engage in formal operations. Instead, they are the foundation for more advanced skills, informing Hilbert's intuition and Wilensky's concretion. Indeed, the abilities of earlier stages can become particularly critical when a student is confronted with something new, for which he or she has few referents. This is the position which Piaget articulated later in his career. While he may never have thought that earlier developmental stages dropped away like the stages of a rocket, he made clear toward the end of his life that previous stages did not disappear, but were present, often in an altered state, in adult learning and cognition. Furthermore, the evidence that students who had mastered formal operations in one domain did not necessarily have that level of skill in other domains convinced Piaget that progress toward formal operations and beyond was not solely a matter of biological age.

Taken together, it is clear that a learner's progression from concrete thinker to formal/abstract thinker is *not so much the development from child to adult, but the development from novice to expert*. Which students can most benefit from the use of tangible things to think with? It is the learners for whom the concepts are most novel, the ones who have less prior knowledge and experience with which to connect the new ideas to which they are being introduced. Thinking with things facilitates concretion, amalgamation, and the grasp of novel formalisms.

So what's a professor to do? Presenting a student with rules and formalisms can lead to a skilled application of rules, but not to true understanding without an accompanying process of concretion, in which the new concept is connected to others, subjected to multiple representations, and interacted with in many modalities. Without the opportunity, and the time, to explore the formalisms with which college students are presented in their classrooms, students' knowledge will remain brittle, lacking in meaning, out of reach, "ungraspable." Connection—concretion—takes time and care, but it is the surest way to a genuine and robust knowledge of the most formal and "abstract" aspects of a discipline. A focus on "coverage"—getting through as much material as possible because it may be needed for future courses or in professional work—can be the enemy of understanding if students are not permitted the time and familiarity to make concepts their own.

Notes

1. Bennett, C. A. (1926). *History of manual and industrial education up to 1870* (p. 68). Peoria, IL: The Manual Arts Press.
2. Arnheim, R. (1969). *Visual thinking* (pp. 154–155). Berkeley, CA: University of California Press.
3. Campbell, R. L. (2006, March 27). *Jean Piaget's genetic epistemology: Appreciation and critique*. Retrieved from http://myweb.clemson.edu/~campber/piaget.html#note31.
4. Campbell, R. L. (2006, March 27). *Jean Piaget's genetic epistemology: Appreciation and critique* (p. 68). Retrieved from http://myweb.clemson.edu/~campber/piaget.html#note31.
5. Flavell, J. H. (1972). An analysis of cognitive-developmental sequences. *Genetic Psychology Monographs, 86*, 279–350.
6. Flavell, J. H. (1972). An analysis of cognitive-developmental sequences. *Genetic Psychology Monographs, 86*, 279–350. p. 286.
7. Flavell, J. H. (1972). An analysis of cognitive-developmental sequences. *Genetic Psychology Monographs, 86*, 279–350. p. 343.
8. Wilensky, U. J. (1993). *Connected mathematics: Building concrete relationships with mathematical knowledge* (Unpublished doctoral dissertation). Cambridge: Massachusetts Institute of Technology, p. 17.
9. Wilensky, U. J. (1993). *Connected mathematics: Building concrete relationships with mathematical knowledge* (Unpublished doctoral dissertation). Cambridge: Massachusetts Institute of Technology, p. 106.
10. Root-Bernstein, R., & Root-Bernstein, M. (1999). *Sparks of genius: The thirteen thinking tools of the world's most creative people*. Boston, MA: Houghton Mifflin.
11. Quoted in Root-Bernstein, R., & Root-Bernstein, M. (1999). *Sparks of genius: The thirteen thinking tools of the world's most creative people* (p. 17). Boston, MA: Houghton Mifflin.
12. Johnson, M. (2007). *The meaning of the body: Aesthetics of human understanding* (p. 270). Chicago, IL: The University of Chicago Press.
13. Heilbroner, R. (1979). Modern economics as a chapter in the history of economic thought. *History of Political Economy, 11*(2), 192–198. p. 198.

14. Arnheim, R. (1969). *Visual thinking* (pp. 306–307). Berkeley, CA: University of California Press.
15. Arnheim, R. (1969). *Visual thinking* (p. 302). Berkeley, CA: University of California Press.
16. Oppenheimer, F., & Correll, M. (1964). A library of experiments. *American Journal Physics, 32*, 220. doi:10.1119/1.1970183
17. Oppenheimer, F. (1968). A rationale for a science museum. *Curator: The Museum Journal, 11*(3), 206–209. p. 207.
18. Merleau-Ponty, M. (1962/2008). *Phenomenology of perception* (p. 352). London, UK: Routledge.
19. Ariely, D. (2012). *The (honest) truth about dishonesty: How we lie to everyone—especially ourselves* (p. 59). New York, NY: HarperCollins.
20. Wilensky, U. J. (1993). *Connected mathematics: Building concrete relationships with mathematical knowledge* (Unpublished doctoral dissertation). Cambridge: Massachusetts Institute of Technology.
21. Turkle, S., & Papert, S. (1990). Epistemological pluralism: Styles and voices within the computer culture. *Signs: Journal of Women in Culture and Society, 16*(1), 128–157.
22. Oxford English Dictionary online. Retrieved from https://www.oed.com/.
23. Wilensky, U. J. (1993). *Connected mathematics: Building concrete relationships with mathematical knowledge* (Unpublished doctoral dissertation). Cambridge: Massachusetts Institute of Technology, p. 58.
24. Wilensky, U. J. (1993). *Connected mathematics: Building concrete relationships with mathematical knowledge* (Unpublished doctoral dissertation). Cambridge: Massachusetts Institute of Technology, p. 52.
25. Arnheim, R. (1969). *Visual thinking* (p. 204). Berkeley, CA: University of California Press.
26. Quoted in Belenky, M. F., Clinchy, B. M., Goldberger, N. R., & Tarule, J. M. (1986/1997). *Women's ways of knowing: The development of self, voice, and mind* (p. 135). New York, NY: Basic Books.
27. Hilbert, D., & Cohn-Vossen, S. (1952/1999). *Geometry and the imagination* (P. Nemenyi, Trans.). Providence, RI: American Mathematical Society Chelsea Publishing. Emphasis in the original.
28. Shavelson, R. J., Ruiz-Primo, M. A., & Wiley, E. W. (2005). Windows into the mind. *Higher Education, 49*, 413–430.

Interlude E: Designing the Future World

Once my studio-style classroom, the Laboratory for Interdisciplinary Design (described in Interlude F), was up and running, I faced the challenge of creating a course that would take advantage of its capabilities. To continue to teach using the half-measures from the days when my students had chairs with wide arms but no tables to build and collaborate on, and when I had to hand carry the physical materials for each class into and out of the classroom, would be to shortchange these embodied learners. Without a fully reimagined course, I would also miss my chance to further explore a thinking-with-things pedagogy, and the fun and surprise that can accompany it. I wanted to embrace sociologist Richard Sennet's maxim, "Making is Thinking."[1]

Building on my experience teaching a social-science-based course on Sustainable Development that a colleague and I had begun in the late 1990s, I created a new course called "Designing the Future World." Inspired by the student who had told me that the project I'd introduced in the Sustainable Development course didn't just teach him about environmental challenges but taught me that "I could *do something* about" the problem, my primary goal for the course was to develop that sense of agency in my students, and give them some tools to aid them in addressing complex social, economic, and environmental problems.

One of the key skills I wanted to cultivate in my students was "design thinking,"[2] which, in its broadest form, is a problem-solving method well adapted to situations that are unique, highly complex, and never permanently solved. In the class, students learned a multi-step process: identify a problem, gather relevant information, describe the problem, brainstorm possible solutions, evaluate solutions, develop the best ideas, construct a prototype of the solution, evaluate and modify the prototype, and communicate their work to others. The process is not linear, and after practicing abbreviated versions of the approach in the first half of the semester, much of my work in the second half of the semester was coaching student teams through the process as they worked on a project of their choice. In this way, my students learned to tackle what the urban planning literature calls "wicked problems."[3]

When the university adopted the Essential Learning Outcomes approach developed by the Association of American Colleges and Universities (AAC&U), I selected "Critical Thinking and Problem-solving" and "Responsibility and Ethics" as the learning outcomes that best reflected my teaching goals. The course was also designated to satisfy the general education social science requirement and the ethics requirement in the computer science department. Because it satisfied several requirements, the course was easier to market to students who did not have an intrinsic interest in the class before they enrolled. Although at first I was miffed with students who told me that they signed up for my class just to fulfill a requirement, I came to cherish these students when I saw them become engaged and enthusiastic participants. While it can be pleasurable to "preach to the choir," I know of few experiences more satisfying than seeing a student light up with a new idea or inspiration. Years later, I was still getting student comments like, "While signing up for this course I thought it was going to be boring and something I would not enjoy. It turns out I was completely wrong in every way possible." One of my favorite comments was,

> When I signed up for this class it was an elective that was just picked out for me. In all honestly before I started on that very 1st Monday, I was about to drop the class and my boyfriend told me to go. Because he felt it would be a class that I would really enjoy and couldn't explain why. . . . After that 1st day I didn't wanna leave. I actually showed up to every class because I really wanted to."

On the first day of class I give my students a handout of the "Five Myths About Learning in College" (described in Chapter 1). I talk about how much more interactive the course will be compared to what most are used to, and I lead them through my introductory Lego exercise ("build a monument/garden/tower" and "build something that expresses how you learn/where you see yourself in five years/your favorite learning environment"). In so doing I give students a taste of how this course will be different, and I also discover a little about each student's personality and their learning preferences. Occasionally a student drops the course after this first class, but more often I have a student ask whether their friend or roommate can also take the course because they think they would love it. One student, in his final course reflection, said,

> the Lego [exercise] where we created our "ideal study environment" allowed us to create something with our hands and share this creation with our peers. This technique of allowing students to teach each other by their experiences and creations is a great way to show that all students are different.

Many of the things I do as a teacher are not original to me, nor do I claim to have done anything close to a perfect job of teaching my students. The course is always a work in progress as I try to find material that is topical and engaging, and replace topics and assignments that are not working well with material I think will work better. Here are a few elements of the course that I think work best.

Hands-On In-Class Exercises

Having used the Lego exercise the first day, in a subsequent class I introduce students to the principles of so-called Universal Design, a design approach that aims to accommodate users with the widest possible range of abilities. Universal Design began in the field of architecture, identifying physical barriers such as stairs and round doorknobs and advocating their replacement with, for example, ramps and lever door openers. Universal Design has now spread to other fields such as education. I challenge my students with a Universal Design Scavenger Hunt, in which students leave the classroom in small groups for 15 minutes and explore the building to find as many violations of the principles of universal design as they can. When they return to the classroom, each group chooses one of the violations they found and makes a quick sketch poster of a redesign that would ameliorate the problem. All teams tape their posters to the wall and we mill around, looking at their designs and discussing them.

Early in the semester I do an exercise in which students use modeling clay. I ask students to respond to a reading I assign about empathy as a design skill by using the clay to model (even in a very abstract way, and in three minutes) something or someone they wish to empathize with. As with the Lego, after they build we go around the room and each student shows their

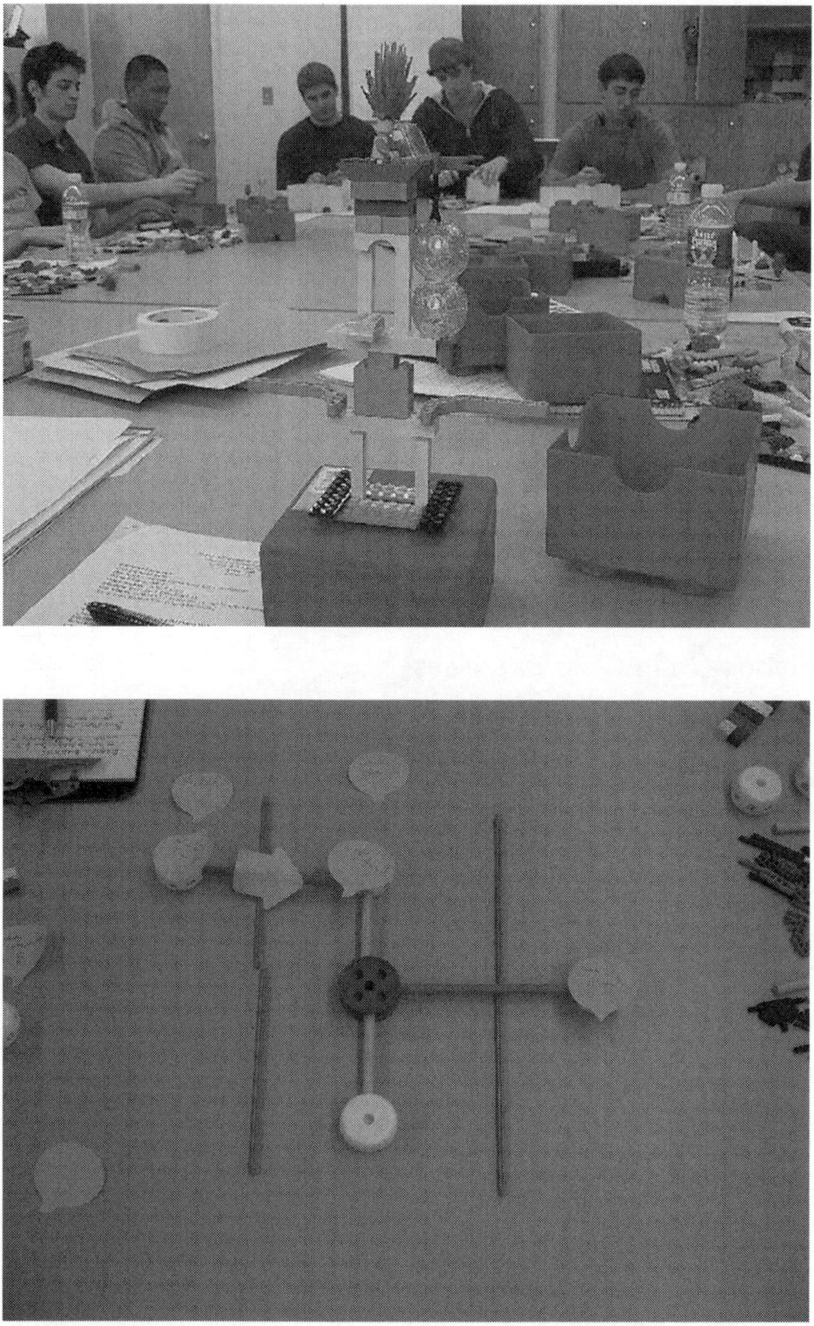

Figure E.1 Quick hands-on exercises in the Designing the Future World class.

clay sculpture and says what it represents. (I tell students before they begin that they will be showing their work to others, so that if something is too personal they can select a different focus). After the exercise is over and the students place their clay back in the plastic package it comes in, I explain that some people benefit from having a low cognitive load activity they can do with their hands while they are trying to pay attention (see Chapter 6 for a discussion of this). I invite the students to take the clay away with them if they want to, or to leave it in a plastic bin I keep near the door so they can retrieve the clay before each class. Every semester, somewhere between a quarter and a half of my class of 24 students take me up on this offer. The only rule I impose is that they not use the clay in a way that distracts them or others during class, because of course this would defeat the purpose.

In the Fall of 2019 I took advantage of an exciting opportunity. The university was opening a research facility called the Fabric Discovery Center, part of a national network to support research and development on advanced technical textiles and their manufacturing. A local organization, the Fashion Makerspace, moved into the building in order to collaborate with the FDC. I was already interested in how textiles and fashion could be a vehicle for engaging students and teaching concepts in science, technology, engineering, and math. To take advantage of this new opportunity, I invited the Fashion Makerspace founding director Diana Coluntino to partner with me in teaching a revised version of "Designing the Future World." For half of every week's three-hour class, we were in a seminar room discussing readings, watching presentations from me and from students, and in general doing the things that required us to work as a group. For the second half of the class we went to the Fashion Makerspace, where students learned to thread a sewing needle, do basic hand sewing, and use a sewing machine. The students embraced the opportunity; although almost none of them had done any sewing before, they threw themselves into it and even brought work home with them when not required to do so. Teaching students to sew in college, except in a fashion design program, is wildly unorthodox, but the students loved it. At the end of the semester they said things like: "I loved the sewing aspect. I now have a skill that makes me a more effective adult, which is rare in college. I was able to make a tie!" and

> [using the sewing machine], I felt it was like I had a hidden talent because I was very good at using it. I am not the best when it comes to quizzes. A lot of people are book smart but don't know how to use their hands when it comes to work.

As a warm-up for the project that would occupy them for the second half of the semester, Diana created an assignment she called "Frankenstein clothing." We asked every student to bring in three pieces of clothing they did not mind cutting up (a recent assignment involved a trip to a thrift store, where they could purchase clothing to cut up if they didn't already have what was needed). The task we gave them, which they worked on during class time over the course of three weeks or so, was to create a new garment from pieces of the three garments they brought in. The results were wonderfully inventive, and the task was achievable even by students who had never sewed before. While creating a new garment from scratch would have required skills we did not have the time to teach them, creating a "mashup" from existing garments was a great way of scaffolding the skill of creating a new piece of clothing, and good preparation for the large project to come. On the final day of class some students displayed, or even wore, their Frankenstein clothes, making evident their pride in what they had accomplished. "I am ecstatic that I can mend clothing when required and make old clothing new by 'Frankensteining' multiple piece of clothing together," commented one student.

Figure E.2 Teaching a student to mend his jeans as a step in learning to sew.

Just in case they were getting overconfident, though, they also had an in-class assignment in which they were divided into four groups. Each group had a single piece of clothing I brought to class—a pair of jeans, a man's dress shirt, a karate jacket, and a short coat—and each student was asked to examine the piece of clothing in front of them carefully and make a drawing. If this garment were taken apart at the seams and each piece laid flat, what would the pieces look like? Once the drawings were completed I collected them and showed them to the class using the document camera in the seminar room. The drawings varied wildly. The lesson was that, while we take clothing for granted, it can really be quite complex, and that it can take very careful observation to understand how a garment is constructed and from what elements.

Learning Exercises

Instead of asking my students to write short papers, I give them near-weekly homework called learning exercises, which ask them to do something, then write a reflective essay of one to two pages about what they have done. These are generally very popular with students, who make comments like,

> giving small individual assignments over the weeks that have us look at something and bring up our own thoughts on it rather than worrying about tests or quizzes made the class a lot less stressful allowing me to actually focus on what we were learning more.

The active learning component, which often involved going someplace in the community, was very popular:

> [I liked] how the learning exercises sent us out in the community. This started a discourse within my family and friend group where we can all talk about the environment and what we can do . . . we were encouraged to speak to each other and be active in our community to find out answers.

When we learn about environmental sustainability and the dynamics of complex natural systems, for example, the learning exercise asks each student to spend four days during the coming week recycling absolutely as much of their waste as they possibly can. I instruct them to keep a journal of what they recycle, where, and how, and ask them to think about what makes recycling easy and what makes it difficult in any given situation. I warn them that they will not always be successful, and that the point of the assignment is to notice what goes wrong, not to achieve perfection. At first I expected some resistance because I was asking for some sustained effort and attention from my students, but I found over the years that this was one of the most popular learning exercises I assigned. Most students already recycle, but even diligent recyclers are taken aback by how challenging recycling can be (Is this candy wrapper recyclable? Why aren't there more recycling bins? Why can't I recycle a pizza box?) Their observations lead easily into a class discussion about the ways in which waste handling is a system with many moving parts, and reflections on what it would take to make change. One student said:

> The learning exercises were fun and eye-opening and allowed for the class discussions to really "hit home." I especially liked going over what everyone did . . . and seeing what we all got out of it. I saw the learning exercises actually mattered.

Often the first learning exercise is "Bad Designs," inspired by the web site BadDesigns.com, created by human factors designer Michael J. Darnell between 1996 and 2010. Darnell describes many badly designed artifacts, from insulin bottles to traffic intersections to baffling glass doors. On each page of the web site is a poorly designed item with a photograph and a description of the problem (Do I push or pull this door? Which type of insulin is in this bottle? How do you turn this on?) Then he proposes a redesign that would reduce or eliminate the problem. I want my students to recognize that most of their surroundings are designed by people, and that some of the frustrations of daily life come from bad design decisions, not individual stupidity. The learning exercise asks them to observe things around them, select something that is badly designed, and create a page similar to the pages on the Bad Designs web site, with an image, a description of the problem, and a proposed solution.

The ability to observe problems and contemplate improvements is a skill I am eager to develop in my students; I view it as foundational to learning to Design the Future World. Learning exercises are deliberately both active and reflective, and they can be tailored to particular versions of the course. When the class met in the Fashion Makerspace, one of the learning exercises, inspired by the anti-sweatshop, anti-fast fashion campaign Fashion Revolution, was "Who Made My Clothes?" We asked students to select one of the actions advocated by the campaign, take that action, and report on it.

Some students chose to write to their favorite clothing brands and ask "who made my clothes?" in the hope of learning where their clothes were manufactured and by whom, under what labor conditions. The goals of the learning exercise were to make students think about how their clothing comes into being, and to increase their sense of agency in seeking information about social justice issues, and then taking action. At the end of the semester, one student still remembered this learning exercise and commented, "I did not expect encouragement for being an advocate such as contacting corporations over how their clothes are made."

Project

Beginning at mid-semester, once we have a lot of design exercises and study of a variety of complex problems under our belts, students select a topic, a "wicked problem," that will be the focus of their project for the second half of the semester. Their objective for the project is to propose a product or other intervention that could potentially have a positive impact on the complex problem they have selected. The students have already learned that it is misleading to speak of "solving" highly complex social or environmental problems; instead I urge them to think about how to nudge things in a preferable direction, which is often the goal of design.

The project has three deliverables, which must be completed by the final class of the semester. The first is a **poster**, on which they explain, using images and text, what the problem is they are addressing, what they propose to do about this problem, and why their proposal is worthwhile. These are made on freestanding tri-fold boards of the sort typically used in high school science fairs, so that projects can be arranged around the room on tables at the open house.

The second deliverable is a three-dimensional physical **artifact**, which may be a rough prototype if they are proposing a device of some sort, or it can be a construction which illustrates or dramatizes the problem. I call them "concept prototypes," which, like concept cars at auto industry shows, express a design intention but are not ready for full scale production. For example, a team focused on reforestation built a small robotic device with Lego and a microprocessor. Their design story was that the robotic rover could travel through the forest, test moisture in the soil with a probe, and drop a seed at suitable locations. At the open house, their prototype struggled a bit even with the carpeting on the floor, but they did have a moisture sensor onboard, and a little robot that could move around. Another team,

Figure E.3 Just before the COVID-19 pandemic, these students created a mask to protect from air pollution.

interested in geothermal heating and cooling of homes, built a small dollhouse and programmed a microcontroller to act as a thermostat. A pair of music majors concerned with plastic waste accumulating in the nearby river collected plastic bottles from the riverbank and made them into improvised musical instruments. In the Fabric Discovery Center, a team concerned with campus safety created a glove that could trigger an alarm and act as a moderate defensive weapon (a scratchy surface on the glove's back) if the wearer were attacked.

The third deliverable is an **elevator pitch**, a 60-second speech that summarizes the problem the team is addressing and the design they created (as if they were briefly in an elevator with their boss and wanted to tell her about their bright idea, which is the origin of the term). By drafting and then practicing the pitch, students learn to boil their project down to a succinct verbal presentation to use with visitors at the end of the semester.

I use a process with near-weekly milestones that guides students through the stages of developing a project, from initial ideas to the final products they will present at a public open house. The process begins with students, in two-person teams, selecting their topic of focus and doing some background research on the problem. In a short meeting with me, we discuss their topic and the approach they are considering taking. Some topics are not well suited to a project for this class—I have had students who are interested in making nuclear reactors safer, or in sophisticated novel technologies for carbon capture. I tell them that, while these are worthy efforts, I do not have the scientific expertise to guide them (nor do they have the expertise to make a meaningful contribution, it turns out when I question them). So what can they do in seven weeks, with the expertise they have or can acquire quickly, that could be a meaningful intervention in a complex problem? I help them to frame the problem in a way that is most likely to be productive and will allow them to converge on a satisfactory result by their deadline. Usually I need to urge them to narrow their thinking (from global warming in general, for example, to the reduction of greenhouse gasses generated by students at the university, or from solving homelessness to supporting the homeless in a specific, local way, in consultation with the city's homeless shelter.) Occasionally a team needs to broaden their thinking. They may be hyper-focused on the pet project of one team member, without thinking about whether it is a good match for the course, the assignment, or the other partner's interest. In that case, I push them to open up and consider alternatives that are still consistent with their interests and capabilities.

The first major deliverable for each team is a two-minute slideshow they prepare and present to the class. In the show they name the complex problem they are addressing, give some facts about the problem, and discuss how they might approach designing an intervention or device that addresses the problem. After each team presents, we have a brief question-and-answer period in which I also give the team feedback. This is the first time that other students get to see what their peers are working on, and they learn by seeing the other projects, and by hearing the feedback given, which often has implications for their own project. In my feedback I model design thinking and ask "what if" questions. I also reinforce the notion that this is a process that can have dead ends, and that as long as you recover quickly from trying something that doesn't pan out, you can learn a lot. In a video that shows an industrial design firm's sometimes chaotic-looking process the students learn that it can be good to fail early and often in order to succeed. I emphasize that any proposal they put forward at this point is provisional and that they should continue to explore and try out ideas.

The next deliverable is a learning exercise with the proposed text for the students' poster, and a description of the artifact they plan to create. Again, I meet with the teams individually for discussion of their plans, giving them feedback and suggestions that can help them over the inevitable hurdles. The last deliverable before the open house is a text of the 60-second elevator pitch they will use to tell guests about their project. During the next to last class, students present their project in class to their fellow students and practice their pitches. All of these milestones give students a sense of progress and sustain their motivation. As one student remarked, "having the Open House gave us a goal for the project just beyond receiving a grade for it and never thinking about it again. I found this motivating and put serious effort into my project as a result."

The final class meeting is devoted to the open house. Students set up their posters and artifacts around the room and visitors drop in to see their projects. Guests wander around, stopping at the students' posters to discuss their projects. While other students, staff, faculty, and even occasionally parents come to the open house, among the most loyal visitors over the past five years have been the staff of the student entrepreneurship program. Their discussions with students are often more substantive, and they also take the opportunity to encourage students to further develop their project as part of the entrepreneurship program. This adds an extra layer of meaning to the "Designing the Future World" course experience because it charts a trajectory beyond the end of the semester and offers support for students who like their project enough to take it further. One student commented,

> I was nervous at first, but after warming up to it all, I enjoyed getting to present our project. One of the guys who visited was intrigued by what we had done, and handed me a business card (which I still need to follow up on).

The open house is the climax of the course—part celebration, part performance, and a powerful learning experience that students will not

Figure E.4 Self-defense gloves created by students focusing on campus safety.

Figure E.5 Students modified a jacket and backpack to create a convertible sleeping bag for a person without housing.

quickly forget. It is not unusual for students to gain a significantly deeper appreciation of what they have done when they see the response of visitors. Projects do vary in quality, but even the weaker projects often come alive at the open house, and I can see the results in my students faces and in the way they talk about the open house in the debrief afterward.

The artifacts students create are especially important as a way to engage visitors and communicate the nature and significance of the project. While some students embrace the creation of an artifact, others resist, but I insist because I have seen the power of having objects to show during what would otherwise be a poster session. The university often has poster sessions of student work across the disciplines, but when I go to one of these I am quickly overwhelmed. Students who have a model or prototype to show get the lion's share of the attention, and my students learn at the open house how valuable it is to present guests with a "thing to think with" and discuss. Students with good artifacts get especially good and detailed feedback. As one of the students in Figure E.5 said,

> I found it very valuable to display our project at the Open House. The reason being is because we had a very good idea. I felt that each person

> that came to our display gave us really good feedback and certain advice and things that we should do to make a product better.

Another student said,

> I found it valuable to display my project because I was able to receive feedback from people that weren't involved in the course. I have a lot of ideas for improvement and I look forward to continuing development on [our] design.

One of the most memorable moments for me was the team that wanted to address the opioid epidemic, and insisted on creating a brochure to educate people about opioids. I pushed them hard—aren't there already a lot of brochures? What value are you adding? I saw that they were trying to attack the problem in its entirety, which is not a recipe for success, and suggested they narrow their focus to an issue such as how to get Naloxone, the overdose-reversing drug, into as many hands as possible. Still they resisted. Then they astonished me by coming to class the week before the open house with a proposal to put doses of Naloxone into the boxes that hold fire hydrants in public and multi-family buildings. Brilliant and eminently feasible. A year later, I heard a radio report that the Veterans Administration was starting to put Naloxone kits in the same cabinets that house Automatic External Defibrillators (AED) for treating heart attacks.[4] AEDs are already widespread in the VA system, and adding opioid-reversal kits is relatively simple and potentially life-saving. I hope my students, who had since graduated, heard the same report.

In students' end-of-semester written reflections on the course, it generally gets very high marks.[5] Most comment on how different the course is from their other courses, saying things like:

> As a Civil Engineering student, I'm used to 50 to 75-minute blocks of grinding through a brand new set of examples each and every class. This course was a nice breather.

> This course helped learn a lot about me and how I can improve my skills mentally and physically. . . . What I mean by that is that it really helps you to think outside the box and be creative and view all the different ways you can you use to solve a problem.

> Honestly, I had a blast. This is my favorite course at UML and I got way more out of it than I would in a regular boring gen-ed. I made

> some good friends and got some great life skills and insight. This was a great bang for your buck course at UML.
>
> This is one of my favorite courses I've ever taken. It was a course about how to learn things and how to think creatively, which is something that college traditionally lacks. I will remember this course.
>
> This course was one of my favorite courses at UML. In Computer Science, almost every answer to a question is either correct or incorrect. This course came at a point in my day where I was exhausted from taking 3 classes earlier in the day, and I could finally relax and contribute my own thoughts to the course, rather than reciting facts.
>
> This class and project was amazing. It was my favorite class I have ever taken in my whole life.
>
> This course has been a great experience, one which I will remember probably for the rest of my life. Not only did we get to look into very real, "wicked" problems affecting our communities and our world, we also got to learn hands-on technical skills like sewing. Taking this class really opened my eyes and inspired me to finding new life for my clothing rather than disposing of it, which I have learned now is a big problem in the world today.
>
> It is a very refreshing and memorable course. The course also reminds me to be keenly aware of my impact on this world. Overall a fantastic course.

Because my aim is to have an enduring impact on my students, and have them remember the course in the years ahead, I particularly cherish comments like, "One thing I liked about this course is that it instilled some new, better habits when it comes to recycling or being more sustainable."

"This course helped give me a perspective for how the technology I will hopefully go on to develop might affect people all over the world," said a Robotics student, who added,

> Automation and machine learning are fields that have the potential for large social changes, so if I want to be on the good side of robotics I will need to consider the social and ethical consequences of my work on a global scale.

Notes

1. Sennett, R. (2008). *The craftsman*. New Haven, CT: Yale University Press.
2. See for example Kelley, T. A., & Littman, J. (2001). *The art of innovation: Lessons in creativity from IDEO, America's leading design firm*. New York, NY: Doubleday.
3. Rittel, H., & Webber, M. (1973). Dilemmas in a general theory of planning. *Policy Sciences*, *4*, 155–169.
4. Bebinger, M. (2018, September 27). VA adding opioid antidote to defibrillator cabinets or quicker overdose response [Radio broadcast]. *WBUR*. Retrieved from www.npr.org/sections/health-shots/2018/09/27/650639122/va-adding-opioid-antidote-to-defibrillator-cabinets-for-quicker-overdose-respons.
5. Yes, I selected these comments, but they were all from the same semester, demonstrating how frequently students give high praise to the class.

6 Embodiment Revisited

"All skills, even the most abstract" says sociologist Richard Sennett, "begin as bodily practices."[1] This observation, arising from his study of craftsmanship, neatly sums up the argument of this book. But before concluding, there are some aspects of embodiment that deserve additional attention because of their implications for learning in higher education. Building on the groundwork laid in Chapter 2, this chapter discusses the role of the hand, the senses, and the emotions in learning. It also raises important issues about thinking with things and student attention, as well as the ways in which we *create* disability in the typical college classroom.

The Hand

A book about thinking with things calls for some extra attention to the human hand, a vehicle for much of embodied thinking. We talk about *grasping* a concept, or being *handy* at something. We follow *rules of thumb* when engaging in skilled practice. Frank Lloyd Wright speaks of Froebel blocks as being "in my fingers to this day;" the German word "fingerspitzengefühl" (literally, fingertip feeling) conveys the sense of having tact and situational awareness—a feeling for one's situation. And the list goes on and on.

These uses draw our attention to the critical and often overlooked role of the hand in embodied learning and knowing. Consider this grotesque little figure (Figure 6.1). Rather than simply an ugly caricature, it is a model that maps the brain's sensory cortex to the parts of the body. Each part of the figure's body is sized in proportion to the amount of sensory cortex devoted to sensing in that part of the body.

In most people, the sense of vision takes up a significant part of the brain's processing power, but there is a separate visual cortex, explaining

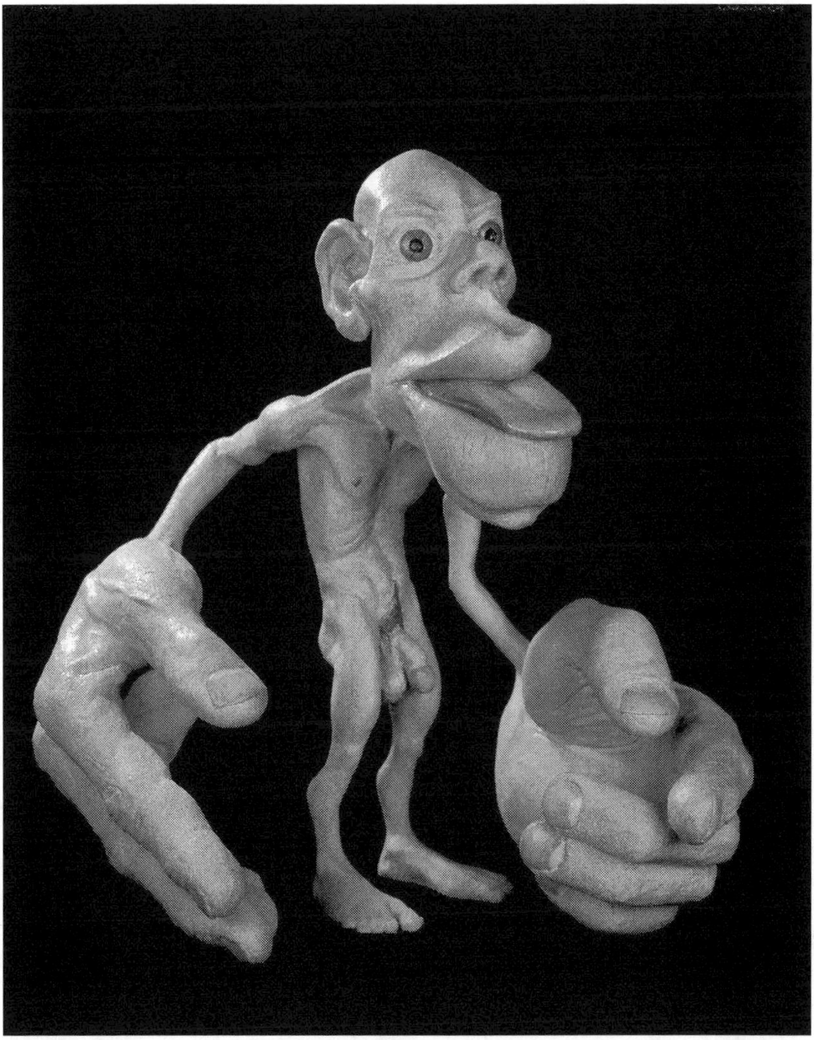

Figure 6.1 A model of a man's body in which each part is shown in proportion to the amount of sensory cortex devoted to that part.

why the eyes of this figure are not overpoweringly large. Focusing just on the sensory cortex, the most striking thing about this figure is the enormous size of the hands, dwarfing all other structures. Why are our hands so copiously endowed with precious space in our sensory cortex? Why would *homo sapiens*, the thinker, the knower, waste so much brain power on the hand? The answer takes us back to the truth that learning and knowing are fundamentally active and interactive, and that the hand, with its versatility, sensitivity, and opposable thumbs, is beautifully suited to inquiry. Manipulation, fabrication, representation, and almost all other human activities involve the hand in some way. As everyone who has had a hand injury knows, we don't appreciate the ubiquity of the hand in our daily activities until one or both hands are out of action. The disabling effect of being without a hand is on display in expressions like "with one hand tied behind my back."

A focus on the hand, though, can miss the extent to which our hands are part of a larger *system*. Typically, we think of our hand as ending at our wrist, but if we peel back the skin we will see muscles, tendons, ligaments, and neural pathways that connect the hand to the forearm, the upper arm, the shoulder, the brain. Where does the hand end and the brain begin? Any spot we pick would be arbitrary, just as the mind/body separation is arbitrary, from a biological perspective. Frank Wilson, a neurologist whose clinical work includes extensive treatment of musicians with hand problems, uses the phrase *hand-brain complex* to express the deep and elaborate interconnectedness of hand and brain.[2]

> If it is true that the hand does not merely wave from the end of the wrist, it is equally true that the brain is not a solitary command center, floating free in its cozy cranial cabin. Bodily movement and brain activity are functionally interdependent. . . . The hand is so widely represented in the brain, the hand's neurologic and biomechanical elements are so prone to spontaneous interaction and reorganization, and the motivations and efforts which give rise to individual use of the hand are so deeply and widely rooted, that we must admit we are trying to explain a basic imperative of human life.[3]

Wilson knows as well as anyone that the muscle memories of pianists, for example, are not stored *just* in the fingers or just in the brain, but participate in the hand-brain system, where habits of mind and habits of body are inseparable. Moreover, Wilson asserts the critical importance of the hand not only in praxis, but also in reason and cognition, which are often thought to reside solely in the brain. "I would argue" he says "that any theory of human intelligence which ignores the interdependence of hand and brain function, the historic origins of the relationship, or the impact of that history on developmental dynamics in modern humans, is grossly misleading and sterile."[4]

The relationship between the hand and cognition can be seen even in such an "abstract" activity as language. There is evidence that human language may have emerged from, and co-developed with, gesture. The neural structures that support language and those that support the movement of the hand have a lot of overlap, and the anthropological evidence suggests the ubiquity of gesturing while speaking, even among the blind.[5] The hand is a wonderful, and ideally accessible, thing to think with.

Like the body as a whole, the hand-brain complex plays an essential role in human meaning making. A primary vehicle for interaction with the world, the hand often leads the way in exploration. In partnership with the visual system, the hand-brain complex (which I shall from now on refer to simply as the hand for convenience) is a key locus of learning through manipulation. In fact, I argue that when we are talking about our human ability to "grasp" a concept, an idea, a meaning, we are not "merely" speaking metaphorically, but are reflecting something fundamental about how human conceptual development takes place. "Understanding is Grasping" is a metaphor which grounds the more abstract idea—understanding—in terms of the fundamental experience of taking hold of a desired object.[6] Pushing and grasping are "included in . . . the action sequences that help develop the object concept" in infants, says Flavell.[7] The presence of the Latin verb "prehendere" (grasp) in English words like "comprehend" is additional circumstantial evidence for the link between holding and understanding. Even the word "metaphor" comes from a root that means "carrying over."

The marriage of metaphor and making is a key feature of *Lego Serious Play* (LSP), a system of facilitated workshops with Lego that promote team-building and strategic planning in organizational settings. Participants build with Lego, at first individually, to represent their perspectives and values, then join their work in a collective construction. By building, then telling the story of what you have built, and finally connecting your construction with that of others in the group, participants express themselves and gain insight into the thoughts and feelings of others in the group. After I had begun using Lego regularly in my classroom I met Robert Rasmussen, a Lego company representative, who introduced me to LSP. I was already primed by my classroom experience to embrace this method, but my horizons expanded as I worked with Rasmussen.

In 2004, Rasmussen and I collaborated on a workshop for professors, delivered at a national conference, on how to use Lego in the classroom (I describe this further in Chapter 7). The workshop was so popular that we were invited back the next year, all expenses paid. In the second year, the workshop, limited to 50 participants, was so oversubscribed it had to be repeated three times to accommodate all the interested attendees. The third year it became a pre-conference workshop with a hefty additional charge. The appetite among faculty for this approach made a deep impression on me.

The creators of LSP see the constructions that workshop participants make as metaphor-creation, a part of a process of meaning making that is essential to the insights generated in LSP workshops. The students who build with Lego in my classroom are also constructing meaning through metaphor. When I give a building task, I often use a prompt that does not suggest that I am looking for a literal model of an object in the real world. Instead, I am looking for a tangible expression of something important to the student which may or may not originate in a physical form.

The hand and embodied understanding play an essential role even in domains like mathematics, which many would point to as the most abstract of all human endeavors. Our mathematical understanding is grounded in the body, and perhaps particularly in the hand. Lakoff and Nunez[8] go so far as to say that mathematics "as we know it or can know it" is a product of the embodied mind. As just one example, research on finger counting provides a window into the ways in which the body both participates in and shapes mathematical understanding and performance. Human fingers are "naturally available and cognitively utilizable"—that is, they are *ready to hand*.[9] Fingers seem to invite number inquiry, and most cultures have finger counting systems of some sort. Research on children with mathematical difficulties has found an association between difficulties in mathematical learning and deficits in what is known as "finger gnosia" (the "ability to locate, name, and discriminate individual fingers"[10]). Children with deficits in finger gnosia had difficulty representing small magnitudes (from 1 to 10) and in "reducing the cognitive load necessary to solve arithmetic problems."[11]

In American culture, finger counting for any but the youngest children is discouraged and even stigmatized, as if it were a sign of serious simple-mindedness and a starkly limited understanding of mathematics. This stigma discourages learners from embracing an embodied understanding of mathematics and reinforces the sense of math as something "other"—abstract in the sense of being distant from the self. Finger counting systems vary widely across cultures, however, as does the social attitude toward use of the hands and body in counting and in performing mathematical operations. Some cultures have sophisticated systems that may, for example, count much higher than the American limit of ten fingers, and may enlist additional body parts—such as the eyes, toes, ears, and shoulders, as tokens for counting.

I first learned when talking to a colleague, Roli Varma, that the simplistic finger counting system I learned as a child in the US was not the only one.

Growing up in India, she learned to count on her hands using the edges of each finger bone (three finger joints plus the finger tip) so that each finger held four numbers, not just one. Using her system, it was possible to count to 20 on each hand, for a total of 40 across both hands (see Figure 6.2 (e)).

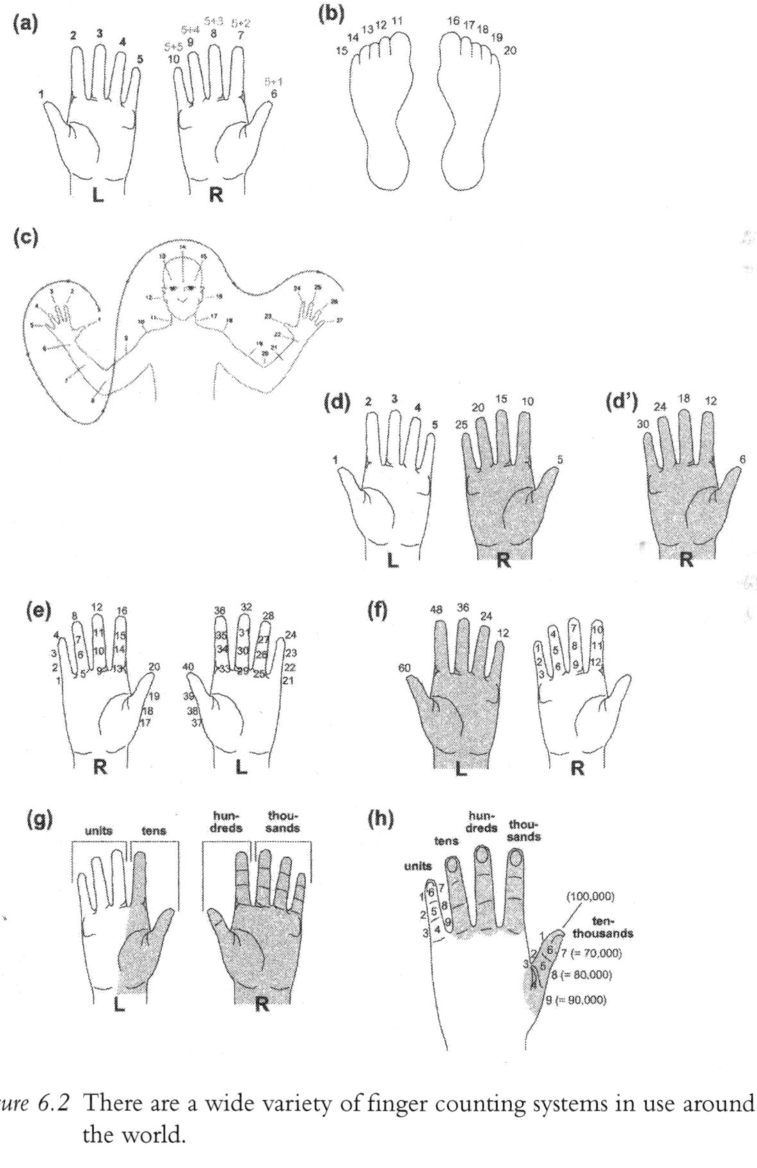

Figure 6.2 There are a wide variety of finger counting systems in use around the world.

Furthermore, it was possible with this system to make calculations. Fluency in this method allowed users to enumerate and calculate quickly in a way that was quintessentially ready to hand. As a result, Varma told me, all Indian children regard mathematics as their birthright. The same cannot be said of American children.

The use of finger counting, and the particular system of finger counting used, has cognitive implications for adult performance on mathematical tasks. Domahs and his colleagues tested adults who had grown up with the same finger counting system I was taught (one number per finger, for a total of ten across both hands). The prevalence of base-ten arithmetic systems in many cultures may have come, at least in part, from finger counting of this sort. But the Domahs team also observed that the presence of five fingers on a single hand creates a "sub-base-five" system in which there is an ever-so-slight cognitive disruption, even in adults, when dealing with magnitudes more than five but less than ten, compared with their fluency in processing numbers five or less. This effect shows up in tiny but measurable lags in response time on simple numerical tasks.[12] Furthermore, when comparing different ways of representing mathematical values—finger counting, verbal systems, and Arabic digit notation—inconsistencies among these systems can have a lingering cognitive effect.[13] For example, the discontinuity of sub-base-five finger counting does not occur in the Arabic numerals 1 through 10, creating a slight mismatch. Verbal systems do not always translate easily into notation (word problems being notoriously challenging for some students, for example). While much research remains to be done, there is suggestive evidence that inconsistencies of this sort may cause difficulties for young learners, and leave challenges even in the adult mind.

The Senses

Another element of embodied cognition that deserves our attention is the human senses as a group. Research on learning in college has shown that using multiple media improves comprehension and recall, but in practice, "multisensory instruction" in higher education usually only means using auditory and visual means of communicating with students. The other senses are left to fend for themselves—and they do, although perhaps in a way that is sometimes at cross-purposes with student learning.

To better understand the problem, consider that although we generally think of human beings as having five senses, our sensory repertoire is actually broader than this common understanding indicates. Beyond the auditory and visual senses, the sense of touch is the one most often explicitly drawn upon in instruction, although only in a narrow range of fields, such as the studio arts, the science or engineering laboratory, and clinical instruction. Although the hand is exquisitely sensitive to touch, it is only one source of tactile information.

> The skin has many different kinds of receptors for receiving sensations of touch, pressure, texture, heat or cold, pain and movement of the hairs on the skin. Although we may not think much about the role of touch in our lives, the tactile system is the largest sensory system and it plays a vital role in human behaviour, both physical and mental.[14]

Our skin is a part of our viscera, and as such plays a major role in the survival-critical function of the homeostatic regulation of the body.[15]

The senses of smell and taste play no deliberate role in most college classrooms, with very few exceptions such as culinary programs. There was a time when medical education included guidance for the clinician in using both smell and taste in diagnosing disease, and some astute clinicians likely still draw on their sense of smell as one factor in identifying maladies, but for the most part these senses are not considered or made use of in higher education pedagogy.

Finally, we have the little-recognized "kinesthetic" senses, which are not included when we talk about having five senses. Nevertheless, the kinesthetic senses are fundamental, and are constantly at work giving us information about the position, movement, and balance in our bodies. Touch plays a role in kinesthetic sensing, along with the vestibular sense, which helps us to balance and to maintain an upright posture. Last, proprioception rounds out the picture.

> Proprioception is our innate sense of "position." We receive information from our muscles and joints through muscle contraction/activation, which helps us know how our body is moving and that our body can do what we need it to. This sense allows us to know our body position without looking—if we close our eyes, we know that our feet are on the floor or we are able to move an arm behind us. It makes us aware of our precise body position in space and enables us to judge grading (speed and force) of movements. . . . Proprioception is closely linked with our other senses, particularly tactile and vestibular, and is a prerequisite for balance, posture, motor planning and coordination.[16]

The importance of the kinesthetic senses in learning is not well understood by most faculty, except in the performing arts and some health professions. Occupational therapists often treat sensory processing problems in children and adults, and may attend to kinesthetic problems. Even when there is no obvious pathology, attention to body location, posture, and movement can have an impact on learning. Occupational therapist Linda Learnard, drawing on her professional knowledge about proprioception and vestibular sense, advised a second-grade teacher to allow children to have the option of lying down while reading. The results were dramatic—children who chose to lie down to read improved their reading performance significantly, the teacher told her.[17]

Rudolph Arnheim understood that every sense, not just vision, played a role in thinking. In the preface to *Visual Thinking*, he acknowledges that the other senses are worthy of similar treatment:

> Perceptual thinking quite in general needs to be considered. Nevertheless, I have limited this book to the sense of sight, which is the most effective organ of human cognition and the one I know best. More comprehensive accounts will have to deal with the specific powers and weaknesses of the other sensory modalities and with the intimate cooperation among all the senses.[18]

Our senses are key to *sense making*. Because cognition is embodied, there is a link between what we perceive and how we think about the objects and ideas in our surroundings. The many meanings of the word *sense* reflect the many connections between our sensations on the one hand and our ability to reason about them, to *make sense* of them, on the other. As philosopher Mark Johnson puts it, ". . . disembodiment is not purity of thought but would, in fact, amount to the loss of all the means we possess for making sense of things."[19] Later he continues,

> Reasoning is not the manipulation of abstract, meaningless symbols according to purely formal syntactic and logical rules. Rather, reasoning is our intelligent-animal way of working through the implications of situations in pursuit of an embodied understanding that allows us to function successfully, more or less, within the problematic situations that we inhabit.[20]

Our embodied sense-making does not even end where our bodies end. We also think with our *environment* in a way far more encompassing than we may realize. Psychologically, neurologically, and practically, our immediate environment is engaged with both our acting and our thinking to the extent that at times it can seem like an extension of ourselves. *Peri-personal space* is the space immediately around our bodies—the space within reach of our hands, feet, and head. It is the space in which we interact with the world, with our tools, with our furniture, with our close friends. Just as the brain and the hand are part of a system, so too are the body and its immediate environment. Experientially, they are intertwined, and although it may seem odd, it is not always easy to distinguish the physical body from the body in peri-personal space. My pen may disappear from my awareness in the act of writing, as I become absorbed in what I am doing; my old car may feel like a second skin as I negotiate a familiar country road or urban obstacles; as I play my instrument or my sport I may feel as if the objects in my hands are a part of me, an extension of my will and my field of action. Scientist and philosopher Michael Polanyi, in his discussion of what he calls "tacit" knowledge, says: "as we learn to use a probe, or to use a stick for feeling our way, our awareness of its impact on our hand is transformed into a sense of its point touching the objects we are exploring."[21] The tool becomes transparent to us, and our attention is now focused, not on the place where our body encounters its immediate environment, but on the place where the tool we are using encounters the world, because that is where the meaningful work is being done. Sociologist Richard Sennett describes the process he calls "embedding," in which, after long practice, a skill becomes tacit rather than conscious, operating in the background. The performance of a skilled craftsman, for example, may seem to be instinctive because a virtuoso has mastered the basics, saving his or her attention for the novel, the essential, the most challenging part of the work.[22] In this way, our embodied cognition extends itself further into the world around us, expanding our reach and therefore also the scope of the peri-personal space on which we act.

Attention in the Classroom

When I first started introducing physical materials into my classroom, I wanted students to use them to express an idea or explore a concept, which they did. What I didn't expect was that, independent of any particular pedagogical intention on my part, my students would also start demanding tangibles for their own sake. I particularly remember an occasion, in an advanced graduate seminar, where I used Lego bricks with my students in a 45-minute "design game." The students seemed very engaged in the game, and during a debriefing they also demonstrated that they had made some interesting and provocative observations about the design process. I was very pleased. But a week later, when they arrived for the next class, they did not find Lego on the seminar table. They protested: Where is the Lego! I explained that the topic for this week did not have a companion Lego exercise, thinking that this would satisfy them. It did not. They insisted that they wanted the Lego. Two of the students, including one who was the most advanced in the class, argued convincingly that doing something with their hands would help them to pay attention, rather than distracting them. With some undergraduates I might have been skeptical of this argument, but this group had proven itself very interested in the subject matter and diligent in doing the reading—a true mark of commitment, reflected in the high level of class discussions. I decided to trust them, and went next door to my office to retrieve my box of Lego. Some of the students were not interested, but others tinkered happily away during this and subsequent class meetings in the semester. I did not notice any decrease in their engagement, and the students who wanted the Lego were quite delighted with the arrangement.

More recently, I taught a seminar for incoming freshmen in the honors program. The university had just instituted this first-year experience for all honors freshmen, but had not given us instructors any detailed directions about what and how to teach, other than that we were to orient the students to the university, make them feel welcome and valued, and introduce them to the interesting city of Lowell, Massachusetts, where our campus is located. Because the history of Lowell is bound up so completely with the history of textile manufacturing in the United States, and because there are wonderful field trip opportunities connected to this history, I focused on the subject of textiles in the class. One week I taught all the students in the class to knit. A few had tried knitting before but most had not. As students on their way to engineering and science majors, some were intrigued. Three students were so excited by knitting that they asked to borrow the materials so that they could continue outside of class. I happily agreed.

At the next class, I told the students they could continue knitting as long as they would promise me that they would not let it distract them from participation in the class. The same three students chose to continue knitting in class, and I noticed an extraordinary thing. One of the students had until then been unusually disruptive in class. This is not a problem I normally have, but this student seemed to feel a need to comment on everything I or anyone else in class said. Sometimes he spoke aloud and sometimes he commented under his breath or to a neighbor. It was annoying, and I could see some of the other students start to scowl at him. I felt like scowling too. But to my fascination, he was one of the students who continued knitting, and he was never disruptive in class again. It was a stark and unforgettable experience.

Finally, and most recently, I gave students in one of my undergraduate classes a hands-on exercise using colorful modeling clay. At the next class, several students asked if I could bring out the clay again. As with my graduate students, they were persistent even after I told them that clay was not on the agenda for that class meeting. By this time, I was primed for the possibility that some of them would say that holding and manipulating clay would help them pay attention in class, so I offered them the same bargain I had offered my graduate students: use it as long as it is not distracting to you or others in the class. Several students continued to grab a handful of clay from the container every time they came to class (and as long as they put it back and I sealed it up, the clay was ready for the next class session). One student said that having others work with the clay in class was distracting her, which we dealt with by changing the seating arrangement and asking the clay users to be quieter, but all in all the students who used the clay said they were happier and more attentive.

When I started telling these stories to my colleagues, several of them mentioned K-12 teachers they knew who taught their students "finger crochet" (crocheting yarn using only your fingers) or knitting to keep them occupied and attentive during class. Some of them had themselves been the students who had been given these materials as children; others were parents of kids with attention problems who were helped by using physical materials in class. There seems to be a lot of anecdotal evidence of the benefits to students of a simple, repetitive, undemanding sensorimotor activity conducted during class time. Very little research has been done on this topic, but what little exists is provocative and suggestive.

In one research study, Andrade[23] asked 40 participants to listen to a mock telephone message inviting them to a party. They were told to write down the names of the other people who would attend the party. The message, which was monotonous and two and a half minutes long, contained the names of 8 people who would attend the party, along with irrelevant information such as place names and the names of others who would not attend. Half of the research participants were given a simple doodling task (shading in small printed shapes on a piece of paper) while listening; the rest were simply told to attend to the message. The group that doodled while performing this fairly tedious listening task performed better than the control group: they correctly identified more of the target names and had 29 percent better recall of names on the tape when presented with a surprise memory test.

Andrade's effort seems to be the first experimental test of the proposition that doodling improves concentration on an auditory task; there is still a lot that we don't know about how and why this works. She speculates that doodling aids attention and memory either by stabilizing arousal levels or by suppressing the daydreaming that arises in the face of understimulation. A person listening to a tedious voice message—or a boring lecture—is prone to mind-wandering, and Andrade hypothesizes that by adding an unrelated task with a low cognitive load, daydreaming is reduced and attention to the main task is enhanced.

The idea that engaging in a secondary activity can improve performance on a primary activity seems surprising. The perils of "multitasking" are often discussed in the popular press, and we know that engaging in activities like texting or talking while driving reduces safety significantly. What is particular about the doodling task, however, is the fact that it is "self-paced, repetitive and involving little controlled processing." The cognitive load is small and time pressure is absent. The doodlers knew they were not being judged on the quality or quantity of their doodling. Their activity is more like fidgeting than it is like planned, effortful action. The resemblance to what my students did with Lego and modeling clay is striking. And the effect of doodling on attention and recall, in situations in which their primary task is listening to speech, is similar to what they report.

Our brains have an *attention system* activated during "goal-directed cognition." We also have a *default* network that is activated when "externally directed thought is absent." Activity in the default system is inversely related to activity in the attention system.[24] If students are sitting listening to a lecture, it is likely that even in the most stimulating of classes their default network will be activated at least part of the time, leading to daydreaming or other distracting activities. Like knitting and modeling with clay, "doodling is a motor act, and when occurring under conditions such as impatience, boredom, and indecision, it seems to alleviate those conditions. This effect recalls other stress-alleviating motor activities such as fidgeting, scratching, and fiddling with different objects." During the impeachment hearings for President Donald Trump in 2020, Republican senator Richard Burr handed out fidget spinner toys to his colleagues, who were faced with mandatory attendance at a trial that would last many hours and at which electronics and other distractions were prohibited.[25] While surely a political statement designed to denigrate the proceedings as unnecessary and boring, Burr also captured a fact of life for anyone who must spend hours on end listening to speeches, lectures, or testimony, no matter how important.

Sensorimotor activities of this sort seem also to have a calming effect on people who are distressed, whether because of trauma, illness, or life stresses. Psychoanalyst Carl Jung used doodling to create "a treatment for neurotics . . . by letting them sketch uninterruptedly."[26] Wernik[27] has used strings of beads inspired by prayer beads in psychotherapy with positive results; fingering the beads and using them as mnemonic devices for patterned and ritualistic repetition of positive thoughts seems to aid patients in creating new ideas and behaviors. Strings of "worry beads," a secular cousin of prayer beads found particularly in Mediterranean cultures, provide a portable opportunity for patterned sensorimotor activity that some people find calming. Manual activities may also help to suppress intrusive thoughts; one research study shows that ten minutes spent making shapes from modeling clay reduces the craving for chocolate.[28] Analysis of reports from knitters around the world show wide agreement that knitting is calming and can reduce pain in patients with chronic conditions; there is some suggestion from research evidence that repetitive movement can release serotonin in the brain, and can reduce the incidence of flashbacks in trauma victims.[29] There may also be a link to creativity; of the artist Alexander Calder it has been said that his hands were always busy, often with a piece of wire. He always had a roll of it in his pocket, for, as he put it, wire was "an easier medium . . . to think in" than any other."[30] The famous Calder Circus at the Whitney Museum in New York is one result of his creative fidgeting.

In higher education, one of the many controversies about which much ink is spilled is the matter of lecturing. Some lecturers are brilliant and endlessly fascinating, but in general, the lecture is a less good way of conveying information if your goal is to promote understanding and retention (which of course is what it should be). I personally abandoned lecturing years ago, using videos, readings, and audio recordings for information that could be laid out through one-way communication. In the classroom, my focus is on interaction, collaboration, making, and coaching. I found I have been rewarded with far higher levels of engagement than I ever experienced in my days as a lecturer. Other faculty complain about their students not paying attention and being distracted by texting their friends in class. In my class this is rarely a problem because my students' hands are occupied with Lego or modeling clay or craft materials, or they are working together in small groups.

In a fit of pique one day, after listening yet again to students' complaints about tedious lectures and faculty complaints about student inattention, I created a symbolic protest which I called The Boring Lectures Survival Kit. I filled a box with fidget toys, a knot-tying kit, a spool knitting set,

Figure 6.3 The Boring Lectures Survival Kit: Some simple materials to improve attention by occupying the hands.

a stress ball, and some simple embroidery, and it sits on my shelf as a silent testament to the unnatural acts we require of our students in many classrooms.

Creating Disability

If I have convinced you that we can regard, as dancer and choreographer Bill T. Jones puts it, "the body as a site of all knowledge,"[31] there are serious ramifications for our classrooms and for how we teach. As I began to understand the implications of embodied cognition, and the extent to which our senses are both ubiquitous and invisible in terms of their role in thinking and learning, I looked around my classroom. I saw the blank walls, the ranks of hard chairs with "tablet" arms for notebooks, and the windows with shades drawn. I came to think of my classroom as a sensory deprivation chamber, in which I was the sole actor, charged with conjuring a world for my students, helping them to make sense in an environment hostile to the senses.[32] I found in Arnheim support for my concern:

> The facilities of the sense of vision are not only available to the mind; they are indispensable for its functioning. If perception were nothing better than the passive reception of information, one would expect that the mind would not be disturbed by being left without such input for a while and might indeed welcome the repose. The experiments on sensory deprivation have shown, however, that this is not so. When the visual, auditory, tactile and kinesthetic senses are reduced to unpatterned stimulation—nothing but diffuse light for the eyes and a steady buzz for the ears—the entire mental function of the person is upset. Social adjustment, serenity, and capacity for thought are profoundly impaired. . . . The continuous response to the environment is the foundation for the working of the nervous system.[33]

Experiments in which subjects are deprived of sight and sound even for a short time show that the effects can include a shrinking of the size of peripersonal space (and therefore perhaps a sense of one's "reach"), as well as hallucinations and other "schizotypal behavior."[34] Fortunately, my classroom is not as empty as a real sensory deprivation chamber would be. At the same time, the sensory deprivation classroom does little to support embodied, sensory thinking and learning. In recognition of this, I've started to issue this challenge: *It's time we came to our senses in higher education.*

What happens when we create an educational system that rejects the evidence of embodied cognition and instead teaches students as if they were "brains on a stick who come to be filled with skills and information"[35]? When we relegate the remarkable human hand, with which our brain has co-evolved over millennia, to simple note-taking? When we create a classroom that is a sensory deprivation chamber? Some time ago I learned from my colleagues in Disabilities Studies that one way of thinking of disability is as *a lack of fit between organism and environment.* Context is crucial. This "social model" of disability posits that the primary location of disability is in society rather than in the individual. While individuals have a variety of characteristics, what turns some characteristics into problems is the structure, attitudes, and priorities of the society in which these individuals live. Although we don't usually think about it, the tallest professional basketball players could be considered disabled because at seven feet tall and more, they don't fit in cars, airline seats, office furniture, doorways, beds, and all the other features of the built environment that assume an average size range. The family dog can hear sounds and detect smells that human owners cannot; fortunately, our survival as a species does not depend on these abilities. Electromagnetic radiation within a certain range is generally visible as light to the human eye. What if a group of people could see electromagnetic radiation outside of that range? They would function far better in a world made for them than the rest of us, with our limited vision and hearing, could.

I contend that some of the students we label as disabled in our educational system are experiencing a challenge we have *created* by designing not for the embodied mind but for the brain on a stick. When we require our students to remain seated, listen to a lecture that lasts an hour or more, and use their hands for nothing more than writing in a notebook, we are creating disability where none need exist. In saying this I am by no means denying the special challenges that some students have, which can benefit from specialized support. Instead, I am arguing that, overall, we have created a winnowing process that favors those students most able to tolerate the sensory deprivation classroom. Unless success in adult life depends on being able to function well in such an environment (and indeed it sometimes does, but not most of the time) we are selecting on the wrong thing. We are selecting not those with the most creative ideas, or the most passion, or even the highest IQ, but those who can best survive a learning environment in which, metaphorically speaking, they have one hand tied behind their back.

Embodied learners are best served by presenting new information and experiences in a variety of ways, using multiple senses. This benefits all learners, not just those labeled "disabled." Experiencing multiple representations of a phenomenon or idea creates a more robust understanding and aids memory. I was inspired when I found an account written by a man who had struggled with dyslexia:

> At the age of twelve, I still hadn't learned the alphabet. Even the "Alphabet Song" couldn't get me past the letter G. . . . The alphabet was displayed on a banner across the top of a blackboard at school, but I couldn't keep the letters straight. They always seemed to be turning upside down, reversing into mirror images or appearing in a different place. . . . One thing I could do was make highly detailed models of things from muddy clay I dug out of a small pit in the back yard. One day, I formed a D, an F, and an O from ropes of clay and left them to dry on the ground. The next day, the D, F and O on the banner at school held still and stayed in their correct places. When I went home to check, I discovered that I had made only one mistake: my clay F was backward. That was easy to fix by flipping it over. . . . I had memorized the shapes of a few more letters that day, so I proceeded to make

> them out of clay. I kept adding a couple of letters each day until I had all 26, arranged in the order they appeared on the chart. Once I had done this, I knew the forms of all the capital letters and their correct sequence.[36]

What if we taught the alphabet, and reading, and writing in a variety of ways to ALL students? What if we taught a sophisticated form of finger counting to math students? Just because I was able to learn the alphabet by sitting at a desk and copying shapes off the blackboard doesn't mean it was the best, or fastest, way for me to come to a deep understanding of these symbols. What if I'd learned math with rods and blocks, as some children do, rather than just with digits and work sheets? What if I'd learned to crochet hyperbolic planes in fourth grade instead of filling out endless multiplication tables? I'm one of the lucky ones who generally did well in school and was never labeled as failing or as having a learning disability, but the absence of those stamps of disapproval doesn't mean that the learning environment was optimal for me. And it certainly doesn't mean that, in the 21st century, it's the best approach for my students.

Emotion

We academics are, I think, deeply ambivalent about emotion in the classroom. On the one hand, we are passionate about our subject-matter, and one of our dearest wishes as teachers is that our students will come to share our passion. On the other hand, as scholars, we are supposed to be "dispassionate," weighing arguments without fear or favor, and banishing bias from our pedagogy and our research. When reason and emotion are seen as opposites, emotion becomes a source of bias, and therefore a treacherous force to be banished from our scholarly engagements. Emotion may be particularly threatening in higher education because we are supposed to have achieved abstraction, that disembodied and timeless ideal of knowledge that is our gift from the Enlightenment.

One of the lessons of the embodied view of cognition, however, is that emotions are key to cognition, and that without them cognition is hobbled or even absent. Before discussing the scientific reasons why this is so, I would like to bring in the voice of Seymour Papert, creator of Logo (described in Interlude D), who is best known for his contributions to math and computing education and for his books "Mindstorms: Children, Computers, and Powerful Ideas"[37] and "The Children's Machine: Rethinking

School in the Age of the Computer."[38] He tells a story from his early years working in schools:

> More than 20 years ago, I was working on a project at the Muzzey Junior High School in Lexington, MA, which had been persuaded . . . to allow a seventh grade to "do Logo" instead of math for that year. [There was an] art room I used to pass on the way. For a while, I dropped in periodically to watch students working on soap sculptures and mused about ways in which this was not like a math class. In the math class students are generally given little problems which they solve or don't solve pretty well on the fly. In this particular art class they were all carving soap, but *what* each student carved came from wherever fancy is bred and the project was not done and dropped but continued for many weeks. It allowed time to think, to dream, to gaze, to get a new idea and try it and drop it or persist, time to talk, to see other people's work and their reaction to yours—not unlike mathematics as it is for the mathematician, but quite unlike math as it is in junior high school. I remember craving some of the students' work and learning that their art teacher and their families had first choice. I was struck by an incongruous image of the teacher in a regular math class pining to own the products of his students' work! An ambition was born: I want junior high school math class to be like that. I didn't know exactly what "that" meant but I knew I wanted it. I didn't even know what to call the idea. For a long time it existed in my head as "soap-sculpture math."[39]

This is a rich little story, with its description of prolonged, project-based work; students' creation of artifacts; and its contrast to dry teacher- rather than student-centric assignments. Most of all, it is a story about emotion in learning. The students follow their own "fancies" as they work on their sculpture; the products they create are coveted not only by their families but also by the teachers at their school; and even a visitor, at the school for a different purpose, is so drawn to the classroom that he wants to spend time there. This is one small but fine example of what cellist Yo-Yo Ma calls "passion driven education." Seymour Papert was in search of similar passion-infused learning in the early days of computing.

Scholarship that focuses on human emotion has only fairly recently become respectable again. Damasio puts it well:

> Throughout most of the 20th century, emotion was not trusted in the laboratory. Emotion was too subjective, it was said. Emotion was

> too elusive and vague. Emotion was at the opposite end from reason, easily the finest human ability, and reason was presumed to be entirely independent from emotion. This was a perverse twist on the Romantic view of humanity. Romantics placed emotion in the body and reason in the brain. Twentieth-century science left out the body, moved emotion back into the brain, but relegated it to the lower neural strata associated with ancestors whom no one worshiped. In the end, not only was emotion not rational, even studying it was probably not rational.[40]

Pragmatists William James and John Dewey did study and write about emotion during the 20th century, but their work was eclipsed in much of the academy by work on such topics as artificial intelligence, which had no place for emotion. Today considerable research is being done, even among computer scientists, on emotion and cognition, but scholars are still catching up with James, Dewey, and others.

Antonio Damasio is one of the leading neuroscientists helping to revive interest in emotion, and to refine our understanding through clinical work, research and writing. In his books *Descartes' Error* and *The Feeling of What Happens*, Damasio makes the case for the important—indeed, essential—role that emotion plays in all human activities, including those thought to be furthest removed from emotion, such as reasoning. Damasio proposes that "the reasoning systems evolved as an extension of the automatic emotional system, with emotion playing diverse roles in the reasoning process"[41] and that

> emotions *marked* certain aspects of a situation, or certain outcomes of possible actions. Emotion achieved this marking quite overtly, as in a "gut feeling," or covertly, via signals occurring below the radar of our awareness . . . As for the knowledge used in reasoning, it too could be fairly explicit or partially hidden, as when we intuit a solution.[42]

He adds that, "Contrary to traditional scientific opinion, feelings are just as cognitive as other percepts."[43] Johnson agrees, saying "Emotions are not second-rate cognitions; rather, they are affective patterns of our encounter with our world, by which we take the meaning of things at a primordial level."[44]

As evidence, Damasio offers extensive clinical accounts of patients, including his own, in whom brain damage that reduces emotion also reduces the ability to think. A patient he calls Elliot had frontal lobe damage following the removal of a tumor, and although Elliot still behaved intelligently, had a good memory, and was able to function in many ways, his affect was flat and he had difficulty making choices and managing his time. While we know that emotion can interfere with reason and good decision making, Damasio asserts that the opposite is also true. " [the] notion that emerges from the study of patients such as Elliot and from other observations I discuss . . .: *Reduction in emotion may constitute an equally important source of irrational behavior*."[45] Furthermore, consciousness and emotion are generally not separable, such that "it is usually the case that when consciousness is impaired so is emotion."[46]

Although Damasio uses the word "bias" to describe the influence of emotion on decision making, he uses it in a neutral way to indicate a predisposition or emotional marker that can have a positive as well as a negative effect on outcomes. He gives the example of a study conducted in his laboratory that involves a game of cards. In the game some decks are good and some are bad; good decks lead to financial rewards, while bad decks lead to penalties. Over time, players learn which is which. Test subjects begin choosing the good decks before they can articulate why; they are also having systematic skin-conductance responses before selecting a card from the bad decks, but not from the good decks. They are showing a nonconscious bias, what might be called intuition. While a game of cards is clearly not a consequential situation (unless you start placing large bets on the outcome), there are many situations in which this sort of pre-conscious knowing could have extraordinary advantages, including survival benefits. So many things of which we may not consciously be aware, or which we may not be able to articulate, come into play in our efforts to survive. "The nonconscious system is deeply interwoven with the conscious reasoning system such that the disruption of the former leads to an impairment of the latter," concludes Damasio.[47]

As a teacher, I have had conflicting feelings about emotion in the classroom. Because my training focused on concepts and promoting reasoning in my students, that was my emphasis as well. I felt unprepared to tackle many topics that are "hot button" issues raising strong emotional responses, and often avoided them, sometimes consciously and sometimes not. It was a shortcoming in my teaching, but it derived from my lack of experience and training in confronting difficult issues. At the same time, I was always attuned to the mood in the room, and had my antennae up to sense pervasive boredom, lethargy, and frustration. I tried to be agile in responding to the mood of the classroom, sometimes by juggling topics or jumping to a hands-on exercise I had planned to do later. Sometimes we just took a quick body break—stand up and wave your arms, walk to the end of the hall and back—the equivalent of baseball's seventh inning stretch. These interventions take time but if my students were growing catatonic, there was no downside to taking a quick break, and it usually helped.

Embodied Knowing

Because in the academy we are often still enamored of the Cartesian view of a disembodied abstract reason as the only truly valuable form of knowledge, we lack the language needed to talk about more embodied ways of knowing. The word "intuition," whose Latin root means to look upon or contemplate, is commonly used to describe the process of arriving at ideas that are not clearly derived from a process of reasoning and logic. This catch-all term, which can be used to refer to the irrational as well as the non-rational, can be accompanied by negative connotation, as with the expression "women's intuition."

Some scholarship in recent decades has attempted to describe and value knowledge that is not explicitly the result of formal and logical linguistic operations. In *The Tacit Dimension*,[48] Michael Polanyi says,

> I reconsider human knowledge by starting from the fact that *we know more than we can tell*. . . . We know a person's face, and can recognize it among a thousand, indeed among a million. Yet we usually cannot tell how we recognize a face we know.[49]

In the same year, Donald Schön, in *The Reflective Practitioner*, considers professional knowledge and the inadequacy of describing skilled professional practice as the conscious application of a set of rules. Instead, the skilled practitioner "draws on tacit knowing-in-action"[50] and exhibits the artistry of skilled professional practice through "reflection-in-action." By this he means that the expert practitioner thinks on their feet, as it were, bringing a wealth of knowledge, including the things that cannot be explicitly articulated, to bear on the problem at hand.

In their book *Sparks of Genius*, Robert and Michèle Root-Bernstein collect interviews and writings by and about many of the leading scientists, artists, mathematicians, and other creative thinkers in the Western canon. Based on their exhaustive research they argue for the centrality of intuition and "gut feeling" to creative insight. The Root-Bernsteins quote Albert Einstein saying "Only intuition, resting on sympathetic understanding, can lead to [insight]" and French mathematician and polymath Henri Poincaré, "It is by logic that we prove, but by intuition that we discover."[51]

Einstein, often regarded in the popular imagination as the essence of the rational genius, was quite explicit about how important embodied, intuitive, non-rational thinking was in his work. According to the Root-Bernsteins:

> Einstein's mental strengths were quite different, as he revealed to his colleague Jacques Hadamard. "The words of the language, as they are written or spoken, do not seem to play any role in my mechanism of thought. The psychical entities which seem to serve as elements in thought are certain signs and more or less clear images which can be 'voluntarily' reproduced and combined. . . . The above mentioned elements are, in my case, of visual and some of muscular type." In a kind of thought experiment that could not be articulated, he pretended to be a photon moving at the speed of light, imagining what he saw and how he felt. Then he became a second photon and tried to imagine what he could experience of the first one. As Einstein explained to Max Wertheimer, a psychologist, he only vaguely understood where his visual and muscular thinking would take him. His "feeling of direction," he said, was "very hard to express."[52]

That embodied, intuitive, inexplicable processes could be the wellspring of intellectual life can be hard to accept. When a creative insight is communicated through an elegant formula, beautiful prose, or a breakthrough design, it is easy to believe that the idea arrived to the thinker in the same medium in which it is presented. Public translations often "clean up" the messy, non-rational underlying process and can mislead readers about the original nature of the creative inquiry. Rote processes taught in school as the "scientific method" mistake the orderly presentations found in research papers (start with a hypothesis, test it, analyze results) for the actual way in which science proceeds. Generally, research papers published in journals hide the sometimes messy, intuitive process that characterizes scientific inquiry.

There is another remarkable process at work in human meaning making, also operating at a pre-linguistic, neurological level, about which we began to learn in the 1990s. Neuroscientist Vittorio Gallese and his colleagues at the University of Parma discovered what they called "mirror neurons" that are part of the primate (and human) sensorimotor systems. Neurons in the sensorimotor system fire when a subject is performing an action, such as grasping a cup. But a subset of the same neurons, the so-called mirror neurons, are also activated when the subject is simply observing another grasp a cup. In this way, they "mirror" in one person's brain an action performed by someone else. They can even be activated when a static image of an action is viewed, or when a cup or other object suitable for grasping is simply visible within reach. Motor activation associated with hand writing has even been found when a person views a hand-written document, as opposed to a printed one.[53]

"*Imagining and doing use a shared neural substrate*," say Gallese and Lakoff.[54] Furthermore, the neural substrate used in action and in imagining are a basis for understanding, they assert. Observing an action, and mirroring it in your own brain, creates a sort of embodied comprehension, independent of, and prior to, language. Our acting intelligently in the world usually involves a process of what they call "embodied simulation." Because of motor neurons, imagining performing an action makes use of some of the same parts of the brain that actually performing that action use.[55] The same is true of watching another person perform an action. This important link between imagination and action lies, for example, behind the common practice among elite athletes of rehearsing, in the imagination, the routine to be performed. In these athletic rehearsals, body movements are minimal or even invisible, but the athlete is creating an embodied simulation, played out over time, of the perfect performance they want to deliver.[56] Embodied simulation might also be the basis for acts of social understanding and human empathy.[57] In acting, as well as in the simulation of action, the meaning of an action can become clear, and can be communicated socially to others. Human meaning, therefore, is not mediated *only* through language and rational thought, but can be transmitted through the mechanism of embodied simulation. Gallese and Lakoff say:

> We have shown how the *sensory-motor* system can characterise a sensory-motor *concept*, not just an action or a perception, but a *concept* with all that that requires. [Furthermore, the] understanding of concrete concepts—physical actions, physical objects, and so on—requires sensory-motor simulation. But sensory-motor simulation, as suggested by contemporary neuroscience, is carried out by the sensory-motor system of the brain. It follows that the sensory-motor system *is required for understanding at least concrete concepts*. We see this as an insurmountable difficulty for any traditional theory that claims that concrete concepts are modality-neutral and disembodied.[58]

Simulation, of course, is not a thoroughgoing substitute for genuine embodied action in the world. It's hard to imagine someone learning to ride a bicycle, or to play the violin, simply by imagining in detail the performance of these actions. But for experts like elite athletes and virtuoso string players, simulation can help embed their planned performance in memory and in action, giving additional opportunities for rehearsal. In the same way, flight simulators and virtual reality battlefields are not full substitutes for the real things, but can contribute to understanding. But before we can fully benefit from simulation, physical experience with actual objects and environments is a prerequisite to understanding and to performance.[59]

Notes

1. Sennett, R. (2008). *The craftsman* (p. 10). New Haven, CT: Yale University Press.
2. Wilson, F. (1998). *The hand: How its use shapes the brain, language, and human culture.* New York, NY: Vintage Books.
3. Wilson, F. (1998). *The hand: How its use shapes the brain, language, and human culture* (p. 10). New York, NY: Vintage Books.
4. Wilson, F. (1998). *The hand: How its use shapes the brain, language, and human culture* (p. 7). New York, NY: Vintage Books.
5. Wilson, F. (1998). *The hand: How its use shapes the brain, language, and human culture.* New York, NY: Vintage Books; Glenberg, A. M. (2007). *Language and action: Creating sensible combinations of ideas. Oxford handbook of psycholinguistics.* New York, NY: Oxford University Press.
6. Lakoff, G., & Johnson, M. (1980). *Metaphors we live by* (p. 20). Chicago, IL: The University of Chicago Press.
7. Flavell, J. H. (1972). An analysis of cognitive-developmental sequences. *Genetic Psychology Monographs, 86,* 279–350. p. 312.
8. Lakoff, G., & Nunez, R. (2000). *Where mathematics comes from: How the embodied mind brings mathematics into being* (p. 364). New York, NY: Basic Books.
9. Bender, A., & Beller, S. (2012). Nature and culture of finger counting: Diversity and representational effects of an embodied cognitive tool. *Cognition, 124*(2), 156–182. p. 157.
10. Costa, A. J., Silva, J. B. L., Chagas, P. P., Krinzinger, H., Lonneman, J., Willmes, K., . . . Haase, V. G. (2011). A hand full of numbers: A role for offloading in arithmetics learning? *Frontiers in Psychology, 2,* 1–16. p. 2.
11. Costa, A. J., Silva, J. B. L., Chagas, P. P., Krinzinger, H., Lonneman, J., Willmes, K., . . . Haase, V. G. (2011). A hand full of numbers: A role for offloading in arithmetics learning? *Frontiers in Psychology, 2,* 1–16. p. 1.
12. Domahs, F., Moeller, K., Huber, S., Willmes, K., & Nuerk, H. (2010). Embodied numerosity: Implicit hand-based representations influence symbolic number processing across cultures. *Cognition, 116,* 251–266.
13. Bender, A., & Beller, S. (2012). Nature and culture of finger counting: Diversity and representational effects of an embodied cognitive tool. *Cognition, 124*(2), 156–182.
14. Jenkinson, J., Hyde, T., & Ahmad, S. (2008). *Building blocks for learning occupational therapy approaches: Practical strategies for the inclusion of special needs in primary school.* Chichester, UK: Wiley.
15. Damasio, A. (1994). *Descartes' error: Emotion, reason, and the human brain.* New York, NY: Penguin Books.

16. Jenkinson, J., Hyde, T., & Ahmad, S. (2008). *Building blocks for learning occupational therapy approaches: Practical strategies for the inclusion of special needs in primary school* (p. 19). Chichester, UK: Wiley.
17. Personal communication, September 2012.
18. Arnheim, R. (1969). *Visual thinking* (p. vi). Berkeley, CA: University of California Press.
19. Johnson, M. (2007). *The meaning of the body: Aesthetics of human understanding* (p. 15). Chicago, IL: The University of Chicago Press.
20. Johnson, M. (2007). *The meaning of the body: Aesthetics of human understanding* (p. 97). Chicago, IL: The University of Chicago Press.
21. Polanyi, M. (1983). *The tacit dimension* (p. 12). Gloucester, MA: Peter Smith.
22. Sennett, R. (2008). *The craftsman* (p. 50). New Haven, CT: Yale University Press.
23. Andrade, J. (2010). What does doodling do? *Applied Cognitive Psychology, 24*, 100–106.
24. Schott, G. D. (2011, September 24). Doodling and the default network of the brain. *The Lancet, 378*, 1133–1134.
25. Coleman, J. (2020, January 23). GOP Senator provides fidget spinners to colleagues at lunch. *The Hill*. Retrieved from https://thehill.com/homenews/senate/479595-gop-senator-provides-fidget-spinners-to-senate-colleagues-at-lunch
26. Adler, A. (1988). On doodlings: The craving for symmetry (M. Cicero, Trans.). *Individual Psychology, 44*(4), 441–443.
27. Wernik, U. (2009). The use of prayer beads in psychotherapy. *Mental Health, Religion & Culture, 12*(4), 359–368.
28. Andrade, J., Pears, S., May, J., & Kavanaugh, D. J. (2012). Use of a clay modeling task to reduce chocolate craving. *Appetite, 58*, 955–963.
29. Corkhill, B. (2008). *Stitchlinks: Guide to our theories so far*. Retrieved from www.stitchlinks.com/pdfsNewSite/research/Our%20theories%20so%20far%20New_%20unshuffled%20watermarked_4.pdf.
30. Root-Bernstein, R., & Root-Bernstein, M. (1999). *Sparks of genius: The thirteen thinking tools of the world's most creative people* (p. 252). Boston, MA: Houghton Mifflin.
31. Bill, T. (2009, September 21). *Jones on NPR's talk of the nation*. Retrieved from www.npr.org/templates/story/story.php?storyId=113032681.
32. Kuhn, S. (2013, Spring). Coming to our senses: Thinking with things in the classroom. *The Atrium: A Journal of Academic Voices*. Retrieved from http://nwi.ivytech.edu/atrium/site/index.html#.
33. Arnheim, R. (1969). *Visual thinking* (p. 18). Berkeley, CA: University of California Press.
34. Noel, J. P., Park, H. D., Pasqualini, I., Lissek, H., Wallace, M., Blanke, O., & Serino, A. (2018). Audio-visual sensory deprivation degrades visuo-tactile peri-personal space. *Consciousness and Cognition, 61*, 61–75. p. 68.
35. Brooks, D. (2018, October 9). A really good thing happening in America. *The New York Times*, p. A25. Retrieved from https://nyti.ms/2E4VFsQ.
36. Davis, R. D., & Braun, E. M. (1994). *The gift of dyslexia* (p. 64). New York, NY: The Penguin Group. p. 64.
37. Papert, S. (1980). *Mindstorms: Children, computers, and powerful ideas*. New York, NY: Basic Books.
38. Papert, S. (1993). *The children's machine: Rethinking school in the age of the computer*. New York, NY: BasicBooks.
39. Papert, S. (1991). Situating Constructionism. In S. Papert & I. Harel (Eds.), *Constructionism: Research reports and essays, 1985–1990* (pp. 3–4). Santa Barbara, CA: Praeger.

40. Damasio, A. (1999). *The feeling of what happens: Body and emotion in the making of consciousness* (p. 39). San Diego, CA: Harcourt.
41. Damasio, A. (1994). *Descartes' error: Emotion, reason, and the human brain* (p. xi). New York, NY: Penguin Books.
42. Damasio, A. (1994). *Descartes' error: Emotion, reason, and the human brain* (p. xii). New York, NY: Penguin Books.
43. Damasio, A. (1994). *Descartes' error: Emotion, reason, and the human brain* (p. xix). New York, NY: Penguin Books.
44. Johnson, M. (2007). *The meaning of the body: Aesthetics of human understanding* (p. 18). Chicago, IL: The University of Chicago Press.
45. Damasio, A. (1994). *Descartes' error: Emotion, reason, and the human brain* (p. 53). New York, NY: Penguin Books.
46. Damasio, A. (1999). *The feeling of what happens: Body and emotion in the making of consciousness* (p. 16). San Diego, CA: Harcourt.
47. Damasio, A. (1999). *The feeling of what happens: Body and emotion in the making of consciousness* (p. 302). San Diego, CA: Harcourt.
48. Polanyi, M. (1983). *The tacit dimension*. Gloucester, MA: Peter Smith.
49. Polanyi, M. (1983). *The tacit dimension* (p. 4). Gloucester, MA: Peter Smith.; italics in the original.
50. Schön, D. A. (1983). *The reflective practitioner: How professionals think in action* (p. 49). New York, NY: Basic Books.
51. Root-Bernstein, R., & Root-Bernstein, M. (1999). *Sparks of genius: The thirteen thinking tools of the world's most creative people* (p. 10). Boston, MA: Houghton Mifflin.
52. Root-Bernstein, R., & Root-Bernstein, M. (1999). *Sparks of genius: The thirteen thinking tools of the world's most creative people* (p. 3). Boston, MA: Houghton Mifflin.
53. Gallese, V., & Lakoff, G. (2005). The brain's concepts: The role of the sensory-motor system in conceptual knowledge. *Cognitive Neuropsychology, 22*(3/4), 455–479; Umilta, M. A., Berchio, C., Sestito, M., Freedberg, D., & Gallese, V. (2012). Abstract art and cortical motor activation: An EEG study. *Frontiers in Human Neuroscience, 6*, 311. doi:10.3389/fnhum.2012.00311.
54. Gallese, V., & Lakoff, G. (2005). The brain's concepts: The role of the sensory-motor system in conceptual knowledge. *Cognitive Neuropsychology, 22*(3/4), 455–479. p. 456, emphasis in the original.
55. Gallese, V., & Lakoff, G. (2005). The brain's concepts: The role of the sensory-motor system in conceptual knowledge. *Cognitive Neuropsychology, 22*(3/4), 455–479.
56. Clarey, C. (2014, February 22). Olympians use imagery as mental training. *The New York Times*, p. SP1. Retrieved from www.nytimes.com/2014/02/23/sports/olympics/olympians-use-imagery-as-mental-training.html.
57. Gallese, V. (2009). Mirror neurons, embodied simulation, and the neural basis of social identification. *Psychoanalytic Dialogues, 19*(5), 519–536.
58. Gallese, V., & Lakoff, G. (2005). The brain's concepts: The role of the sensory-motor system in conceptual knowledge. *Cognitive Neuropsychology, 22*(3/4), 455–479. p. 468. Emphasis in the original.
59. Gallese, V. (2009). Mirror neurons, embodied simulation, and the neural basis of social identification. *Psychoanalytic Dialogues, 19*(5), 519–536.

Interlude F: The Laboratory for Interdisciplinary Design

Decades ago, I took part in an experiment in teaching software development using methods of instruction borrowed from studio courses in architectural education. A group of undergraduate and graduate students at MIT worked on digital projects in a class led by William Mitchell, Dean of Architecture and Planning, and Mitchell Kapor, founder of Lotus Development Corporation, a major software company. Using rapid iteration, frequent critique of student projects, the study of important precedents, multiple media for display and communication, and other methods characteristic of studio education, students worked on a complex, open-ended assignment in which they were asked to reinvent the community newspaper for the digital age.

The class was instructive both for its successes and its limitations. In the years that followed I published two papers about the experiment[1] and gave numerous talks in a variety of venues, including university and corporate settings. I learned a tremendous amount from the class, but was limited in applying it to my own teaching because I did not have an appropriate space where students could collaborate on tables, search the Internet together, and have access to drawing supplies for sketches and craft materials for prototypes. I wanted to explore studio methods in my own teaching, and take what I'd learned from the MIT class to the next level, but was constrained by the conventional classrooms to which I was invariably assigned.

Determined to find a way to bring the studio approach to teaching into the decidedly non-studio social sciences, I drafted a proposal to the university's provost. I had identified a promising space in the basement of the oldest building on campus. Although the room had expansive windows and was in a large, historic stone structure, the building had suffered from years of neglect and the basement room was being used for storage, including a pile of broken furniture dumped in the center of the room by the custodians. The plaster was falling down and cobwebs were everywhere, but I could see its potential and I knew that my request was far more likely to be granted if I was asking for space not currently "owned" by another faculty member. If you commit to making this space into an attractive, usable "white box," I told the provost, I will fit it out with furniture, tools, and supplies. To my delight, he agreed.

I called the space "The Laboratory for Interdisciplinary Design" as a way to market an unusual experiment to colleagues in a technologically oriented university. Furniture and lab benches were scrounged from the cast-offs of other departments. One end of the room had cabinets and shelving for tools, craft materials, and student work-in-progress. In the middle of the Lab were tables that could be pushed together to form a single large table for a seminar-style discussion, or pulled apart for breakout work. Around the periphery of the room were lab benches which held computer work stations (this was in 2005, when most students did not have Internet-connected devices in their pockets and backpacks) and soldering irons. There was a digital projector that used a blank white wall for a screen. On the shelves were hand tools like scissors and screw drivers, construction paper and other craft materials, kits with simple microprocessors, a glue gun, and a variety of construction toys, as well as books and objects designed to provoke inquiry and inspire making.

Because the Lab was available for use by any faculty member who wanted to teach there, I held a number of open houses in the space, and also invited faculty and staff to have meetings in the room when it was not in use for teaching. One of the most gratifying experiences was seeing the faces of some of the faculty visitors. Their eyes would light up as they entered. They'd say, "I'd love to teach in a space like this," or "A breath of fresh air." One professor commented on how great the room smelled! (Perhaps fresh paint? I was never sure) Over time, quite a few colleagues did teach in the Lab, and one who moved his class to the Lab after the semester had started wrote me an email saying,

> It already has changed my teaching—Thursday's class was much better in terms of discussion and human contact. I used the Lego as a way of transitioning them away from computers. . . . I've been telling everyone it's the best classroom on campus and I truly believe that!

Another reported that she had grown significantly as a teacher as a result of using the Lab and understanding its rationale. To truly use all the capabilities

Figure F.1 Scenes from the Laboratory for Interdisciplinary Design studio-style classroom.

Figure F.1 (Continued)

of a space like this requires a faculty development initiative, because major changes in pedagogy take careful thought and planning. Having an enabling space is a necessary but insufficient condition for a significant change in pedagogy.

Over the years there were some upgrades made to the room, most of them not solicited by me but demonstrating the support that others wanted to show for the space. The dean bought new tables and chairs, a brand-new digital projector was attached to the ceiling, a screen was installed, and an instructor's computer with multimedia capabilities placed on one of the lab benches, with a document camera beside it. New Mac computers arrived. The aesthetic I was aiming for when I created the room was a space that was bright and clean while also being slightly scruffy, giving it a "do touch" ethos. Don't worry about your marker bleeding through the paper, or making a small ding in the table when you are hammering. A drip of solder on the lab bench? It's ok . . . that's what the benches are there for. The new furniture did not change the essence of the place: it still read as a place for making things.

I brought in a few small house plants and a coffee maker. The idea was to make the room feel homey and alive. After a couple of semesters, I started a "coffee club." If a student paid $5 at the start of the semester, they could have unlimited cups of coffee during class time. From a collection of mismatched ceramic mugs a student could select one and put their name on it using a marker and a piece of masking tape. It was theirs for the semester, which meant I didn't have to either provide paper cups and a larger trash barrel, or wash student mugs after every class.

A lock with a numeric keypad was also added to the Lab door, and students were given the key code during the first class. I posted the schedule of classes on a bulletin board outside the door and told students that they were free to come into the room to study, work on their projects, or just take a break anytime there was not a class going on in the room. I wanted my students to feel like welcome guests, relaxed and at home in their learning space. Feedback from students after each semester suggested that I was largely successful. It's rare in my experience to have students review the room as well as the instructor and the teaching methods, but positive comments on the Lab were commonplace.

After a long run (from 2005 to 2018) the Lab for Interdisciplinary Design was closed because the beautiful old Beaux Arts building in which it was housed was finally getting its long-overdue renovation. But a measure of its success is that, as the planning was being done for the renovated and expanded building, the committee overseeing the renovation made sure that a successor space would be created to house the next 13 years of invention in teaching and learning. The "Innovation Space" will retain many of the hands-on features of the old Lab and add some new digital communication and construction capabilities. While opening of the space has been delayed by the global pandemic, the thinking-with-things approach to learning in higher education will live on.

Note

1. Kuhn, S. (1998). The software design studio: An exploration. *IEEE Software, 15*(2), 65–71; Kuhn, S. (2001). Learning from the architecture studio: Implications for project-based pedagogy. *International Journal of Engineering Education, 17*(4–5), 349–352.

A Vibrant Learning Ecosystem

7

In the preceding chapters, I have worked to make the case that we must question the conventional way of teaching: lecturing about "abstractions" to seated, immobile students in a sensory-deprivation classroom. The things that many of us already do to go beyond the canonical way of teaching—class discussion, using images, showing films, forming breakout groups—help to make our classrooms more educative for our students. But we can go much further, taking to heart the reality of embodied cognition, the role of emotion in reason, and the fallacy of transmitting abstraction directly into students' heads. How might we go beyond our current patchwork of efforts and remake college learning in the true image of our students' ways of knowing?

Student learning is really what is at stake here, and central to the concerns of this book. Early in my teaching career I remember going to a talk by a scholar from a distant university, who said something I have never forgotten: "If the student has not learned, the teacher has not taught." That has been a core belief for me ever since, although it sets a high standard I have often failed to meet. For faculty, showing up to class and offering up a heaping serving of information is not enough; we must instead start from the embodied student and what will best promote their learning. A student-centered approach to teaching has been advocated by many before me. What I have hoped to show is that by keeping in mind the needs and capabilities of embodied learners we can go even further in promoting student learning.

When I think of the college of the future, ecological metaphors come to mind. Because learning is the interaction of organism and environment, I imagine classrooms that have been transformed into learning ecosystems, where students are inspired to perform natural, rather than unnatural, acts of insight and meaning-construction. Students in these environments draw on the materials around them, their fellow students' actions and insights, and the responsive coaching of their teacher, eliciting new insights and inquiry. The goal is a vibrant learning ecosystem that promotes intellectual and human flourishing in both students and their instructors.

In this chapter I make four recommendations for change in our default modes of college teaching. None of these recommendations is entirely novel, nor do they, collectively, cover all of the challenges we in higher education face. Instead, I have selected what I believe to be the most important recommendations for change, enhanced by an understanding of what thinking with things can bring to college teaching and learning. Happily, most of these recommendations can be implemented, at least on a very small scale, by individual faculty, although adopting these recommendations at the level of the department, the college, the university, or even at the state or national level is of course an even more powerful intervention.

Recommendation One: Promote Thinking With Things to Enhance Learning

Presenting information to students in multiple ways using multiple media helps to deepen their learning and make it more robust. Offering students a variety of representations of the same concept or phenomenon allows them to grasp it in different ways, rather than investing in a single static view. Although the notion that multiple representations are valuable in teaching is already widely accepted, in practice the representations often include only language (written and spoken) and images on classroom screens or in textbooks.

I recall a comment made to me years ago by a smart personal trainer at my gym: "I wish they had taught us high school physics in the weight room. I might have understood it better." This is the central insight of Frank Oppenheimer's Exploratorium, discussed in Chapter 5. At my children's school, high school physics students take a field trip to an amusement park, where they experience the forces described in their textbooks by riding the roller coaster. We can create everyday versions of this embodied experience in our classrooms by using multiple media, including physical objects, in classroom instruction. In so doing, we will give students a more robust grasp of the material we want them to master.

Mathematician David Hilbert praised the value of abstraction in mathematics for its ability to "crystallize the *logical* relations," but also emphasized the importance of "*intuitive understanding* [which] fosters a more immediate grasp of the objects one studies, a live *rapport* with them, so to speak, which stresses the concrete meaning of their relations."[1] In the college textbook *Experiencing Geometry*,[2] authors David Henderson and Daina Taimiņa not only quote Hilbert but also seek to build intuitive understanding in students by having them use physical materials in class to better learn the material. To learn about geodesics on cones, for example, the student creates a paper cone and then experiments with laying a ribbon or strip of paper on the cone to answer such questions as "is the shortest distance always straight?"

In computer software development, the advent of "object oriented" programming required both experienced and novice programmers to dramatically change their approach to designing systems. Ward Cunningham developed an approach he called "CRC" cards (Class, Responsibility, and Collaboration). Although the original CRC cards were digital, Cunningham and his collaborator Kent Beck soon switched to 4" by 6" paper cards, which "give the learner who has never encountered [software] objects a physical understanding of object-ness."[3] Programmers might point to, pick up, move, or even wave a card around in the course of a collaborative design session. Cards could easily be annotated, revised, or replaced by any of the participants, and Beck and Cunningham observe that paper cards were most valuable when a design was incomplete or poorly understood. "We were surprised at the value of physically moving the cards around." This clear value "has led us to resist a computerization of the cards."[4]

The value of CRC cards illustrates a more general point about representations: high fidelity representations and models are not necessarily more valuable than low fidelity tools. In the case of the CRC cards, their simplicity and ease of use was the source of their value. Indeed, more complex and therefore more "realistic" representations might have obscured the most salient features of the programming task, creating distractions for the team. More generally, software developers who were testing the usability of designs intended for non-programmers found that they got equally valuable feedback when users were given either high or low fidelity prototypes.[5]

We can extend this insight to the domain of so-called "educational technology" in general. In the 21st century, there is a tacit assumption that the best educational technologies are digital, and that students learn best on computers and other digital devices. While digital "things to think with" have significant value, it is essential that we embrace the benefits of low-tech materials first and foremost. For novices, digital tools are like abstractions: valuable as novices make progress on the road to becoming experts, but lacking important physical qualities essential to constructing a well-grounded understanding. For the price of one computer, a school can outfit an entire classroom with craft supplies and simple hand tools. The educational value of these "lowly," low-tech materials must not be overlooked.

One of most important objectives of instruction is "transfer," the ability of students to take concepts learned in one context and use them in a different context. Textbook learning, with its "tame" examples presented in static form, may enable students to pass the test but may not adequately support them as they try to apply their knowledge in situations that look dissimilar from those in the textbook. Robust learning allows students to see new situations as cases of concepts they have learned, and apply those concepts in new contexts. The use of multiple examples in instruction has been shown to improve the ability of students to transfer their learning,[6] and it seems highly plausible that varied examples using manipulatives and different media—thinking with things—would enhance this effect.

Physical materials are also useful for allowing students to create their own representations of the concepts they are trying to learn. Often learners are presented with canonical representations (the standard presentation of the periodic table in chemistry class, for example) but are not asked to create their own representations. A colleague asks her music education students to abandon the standard Western musical notation system they have learned and create a novel system of musical notation. Her students must jettison what they think they already know and start over from first principles, considering the characteristics that are most important for them to represent with their new notations. My students, asked to sketch a sustainable community with Lego, revealed what they found to be the most salient features of the built environment, to my dismay. In both cases, students create representations that make their thinking visible to themselves, to their instructor, and often to their fellow students.[7] In this way, thinking with things supports not only inquiry but also communication.

In a workshop I gave for faculty at a conference on improving college teaching, I asked several groups of six attendees each to work together to create a concept map with Tinkertoys and sticky notes. I was expecting two-dimensional layouts of nodes and lines on tabletops; what I was not expecting was that one group noticed that they could create a three-dimensional map because Tinkertoys can be used for three-dimensional building. I was surprised and intrigued. What *is* a three-dimensional concept map? What new meanings or relationships does it suggest? This group noticed the affordances of the materials they were working with and used them to create a new idea. The back-and-forth between individuals or groups and the

Figure 7.1 Two professors of education at a Lego workshop for faculty.

materials they are using to represent their ideas can itself be generative of new insights. By supplying learners (even faculty!) with a variety of materials, we support engagement, active learning, and creativity.

Recommendation Two: Create Conducive Learning Environments

When I was a young faculty member, I was also a mother of young children. I remember going to my kids' parent-teacher conferences and admiring the colorful classrooms in which they were learning. The walls were filled with bright teaching materials, student work, inspiring mottos, and interesting images. Each teacher had their own classroom and used the space and decor to introduce and reinforce the lessons they wanted to teach. To an extent, their classrooms also reflected the teacher's personal style and philosophy. Some had live animals, some had plants, all had teaching materials ready-to-hand.

My situation was entirely different. In the early 1990s, the only things in my classroom were chairs for my students and a desk and chair for me. Want to show slides? Carry an overhead projector up two flights of stairs. Want a wall-sized map? Put in a work order, figure out how to pay for the map, and hope that something good happens. Next semester, try as hard as you can to be assigned to the same room, which will still contain your map if you are lucky.

Fortunately, things are better now. At my university, every classroom has a screen, a ceiling-mounted digital projector, a computer (and a place to plug in your own laptop if you prefer), an Internet connection and the ability to play DVDs or stream videos, and a document camera for projecting a printed page onto the screen. What we faculty still don't have is a meaningful opportunity to personalize the generic university classroom, or to store teaching materials in the rooms to which our courses are assigned.

By contrast, the studio classroom I created (described in Interlude F) is full of things to think with. Lego, poster board, glue guns and glue sticks, markers, construction paper, pipe cleaners and straws, soldering irons, microprocessors and sensors, construction toys, modeling clay: there is a bounty of materials to support exploration, design thinking, and communication of ideas. Abundant natural light, the presence of green plants, and comfortable reconfigurable furniture reinforce the idea that this is a space for the flourishing of John Dewey's body-mind. Dewey wrote that educators should recognize "what surroundings are conducive to having experiences that lead to growth."[8] My experience in this classroom has convinced me that an environment such as this is indeed conducive to student growth and to "the having of wonderful ideas."[9]

This studio classroom I describe in Interlude F was inspired by the spaces where studio art classes take place. Art studios are places where aesthetic judgements and the manipulation of materials—thinking with things—are central to the learning that students do. They are places where teaching materials are abundant and making, both of artifacts and of meaning, is taking place. By foregrounding studio learning I am also giving the arts a central if surreptitious role in learning across the disciplines. To be clear, I am not saying that my students are taking an art course. They are not. But they are drawing on the fundamental embodied sensory experiences that are the lifeblood of the arts, as well as of all human cognition. Just as we have marginalized the body in higher education, the arts have also become marginalized amid the stress on employment-related skills. As Rudolf Arnheim observed,

> The arts are neglected because they are based on perception, and perception is disdained because it is not assumed to involve thought. In fact . . . the arts are the most powerful means of strengthening the perceptual component without which productive thinking is impossible in any field of endeavor.[10]

Much later he continues, "Once it is recognized that productive thinking in any area of cognition is perceptual thinking, the central function of art in general education will become evident. The most effective training of perceptual thinking can be offered in the art studio.[11]

Comments from faculty colleagues who were seeing the studio classroom for the first time showed that they were intrigued and, sometimes, inspired. They often said, "I'd love to teach in a space like this," remarking on the natural light, the coffeemaker, the shelves full of supplies, the colorful student work displayed around the room, and the general informality of the environment. Several went so far as to request to teach in the space, and continued to teach there over the course of several semesters. The studio classroom suggests a new way of teaching and of being, and although their own education and their teaching up until that time had been more traditional, they were drawn to this new environment and its possibilities. Several of my colleagues also joined me in a Thinking with Things faculty learning community which met monthly and discussed teaching strategies, curriculum, and educational research.

When I think of a vibrant learning ecosystem, one of the things I think about is the 17th-century precursor to the museum, the "cabinet of curiosities." Some members of European nobility and other wealthy individuals filled a room with rare and fascinating objects, often from the natural world but also exotic human-made creations. These objects were "curiosities," but were also intended to *provoke* wonder and curiosity in their viewers. Was this a unicorn horn (or a narwhal tusk)? Where did this amazing stuffed creature come from and how did it live? Is that really how an ostrich skull looks? These objects stimulated reflection in the privileged, and gave a sense of the wideness of the world even to those of the elite who never strayed far from home.

A college classroom can be a curated 21st-century cabinet of curiosities, providing students with engaging, provocative things to think with. The most enchanting example of this I have seen is at the Rhode Island School of Design, where the Edna Lawrence Natural History Collection is housed in the Nature Lab. In the main room, the walls are lined with cabinets filled with natural history specimens—bones, shells, taxidermy, stones, and many other things—which students can use to examine and to sketch. Classes meet in the Nature Lab, and students can come on their own to explore the vast collection of things to think with. I first encountered the Nature Lab when my conference workshop on how to crochet a hyperbolic plane was assigned to the space (Figure 7.2). The resemblance of the crocheted planes to the coral structures in the cabinets gave a deeper meaning to the hand work in which we were engaged.

At a practical level, universities can do several things to lay the groundwork for engaging, embodied learning. First, classrooms should have cabinets (you can't have a cabinet of curiosities without a cabinet) in which faculty can have access to a basic suite of physical teaching materials, and can store their own materials for use in class. Classrooms should also have moveable tables and chairs (try making something using just those tablet-arm student seats) for reconfiguring the classroom. The rearrangement of the classroom can even become a design exercise, in which students debate

Figure 7.2 Conference participants learn to crochet hyperbolic planes at the author's workshop in the Edna Lawrence Nature Lab at the Rhode Island School of Design.

the benefits of different classroom arrangements and collaborate in trying new furniture layouts, perhaps even evaluating their choices periodically over the course of the semester. How about "furniture bricolage" (recall Levi-Strauss in Chapter 3) in which pairs of students experiment with scraps of paper, representing tables and chairs, on a scale drawing of the classroom's dimensions? In my class I've had students do this, present their proposal to their fellow students, and then put the designs to a vote. All of this serves not only to improve the classroom but to give students a sense of agency and an appreciation of the fact that classroom arrangements reflect a choice, not a law of nature.

Second, facilities personnel and faculty representatives should work together to collaboratively design teaching spaces. The two groups have different priorities, incentive structures, and it is only through collaboration that classroom configurations that take into account the needs of both groups can be achieved. Of course I believe that the purposes of teachers, and of student learning, should take priority when classroom space is being designed, but issues of cost, ease of maintenance, security, and accessibility are all important as well. My own experience conferring with facilities staff has taught me that, in general, they are eager to support student learning wherever possible, and that they appreciate the respect shown them by bringing them into the conversation about the university's core function.

Third, institutions should allow groups of faculty with shared teaching interests to lay claim to particular classrooms, where feasible, and jointly outfit those rooms with the furnishings and teaching materials they need. These groups might be disciplinary groups, or, perhaps more interesting, groups that cross disciplines but can use things to think with as bridges that unite their varying perspectives. Classrooms in which faculty feel a sense of ownership, even if for a semester, can be more welcoming, can promote collaboration within and across disciplines, and can better support the learning that takes place there. In my studio classroom, I put green plants on the windowsills, to signal that this was a place for growth and flourishing, and also to show that someone was caring for the space (nothing says neglect like a dead plant!).

Overall, schools should work to create classrooms that are the antithesis of the sensory deprivation chamber: vibrant, engaging ecosystems in which embodied learners can flourish, along with their teachers. There is no better argument for place-based education, and no better justification for face to face learning on a physical campus.

Recommendation Three: Educate for Action

If the life of the mind really is the life of the body-mind, then we must think of learning as something that acts in the world, rather than sitting happily inside the educated cranium. If a thinking-with-things approach to learning only prepared students to retrieve facts, rather than to act knowledgeably in the world, it would be a brittle thing indeed. Deep, robust knowing, of the sort that students achieve when they can truly "grasp" the concepts and situations with which they are presented, prepares students to use what they have learned to act in the world.

As we have seen, a conventional but outdated view of education is that students are like storehouses or banks, to be filled up with valuable knowledge that they can withdraw in the future, as needed. At the time of their instruction, students receive homework that asks them to practice the new skills in carefully defined, tame settings. After that, the storehouses are often let alone, their contents growing dusty and illegible with age. This is a good description of my mathematics education in US schools: I waded through years of decontextualized instruction in subjects like matrix algebra, which I did finally see again more than a decade later in an advanced statistics course in graduate school. By then the layers of dust were so thick it was as if I was seeing it for the first time. And although I took several statistics courses, they too were generally quite without context. I learned how to identify a variable and write an equation for a regression, but did not learn when it was and was not appropriate to use these tools.

When I began my teaching career, I struggled with how to avoid replicating the experience I had as a student. The fact that I was not teaching math helped, of course, but I still struggled with how to connect my students' existing knowledge, commitments, and aspirations with the subject-matter I was to teach them. Over the years I developed a number of strategies, but a thinking-with-things approach was one of the most powerful. It made my students' thinking visible to me and to their classmates, sparked conversation and reflection, and made them into active designers of their in-class creations.

I have come to believe that my primary job as a teacher is to prepare my students for intelligent action in the world. If knowledge sits inside the skull but cannot be put to some kind of use in the world, our students may be better able to entertain themselves on a desert island, but will be poorly prepared for full human participation in the dynamic, challenging environment that is their world. Laying the groundwork for action, by posing complex problems and promoting active learning in the classroom, creates a sense of agency among students and builds their capacity for knowledge-in-action.[12]

Philosopher Gilbert Ryle[13] made the distinction between "knowing that"—in other words, propositional knowledge that can be stated as fact—and "knowing how," a form of knowledge that cannot necessarily be articulated, but that is critical to informed action in the world. If knowledge consisted only of "knowing that," perhaps the storehouse model would be an appropriate guiding metaphor for education. But if we believe that the most important forms of learning enable students to act intelligently in the world, combining "knowing that" with "knowing how," then the storehouse model, with its absorption and regurgitation of facts, does a profound disservice to learners.

One area of education where it is accepted that knowing how, and knowing-in-action, are key is in the preparation of students for the professions. Future doctors, lawyers, physical therapists, engineers, clinical psychologists, and a host of others, need to know how to act in a professional manner, not just recite the details of a law or the location and function of a body part. Future professionals spend considerable parts of their training in internships, mock trials, supervised interactions with clients, and quasi-apprenticeship situations. Yet it is this very appreciation of application that has led the professions, and professional schools, to have an uneasy existence in the academy.

Those who cherish the life of the mind may perceive the professions, with their emphasis on practice, as sullied rather than pure, as instrumental rather than disinterested. As Louis Menand trenchantly puts it, "The divorce between liberalism and professionalism as educational missions rests on a superstition: that the practical is the enemy of the true. This is nonsense."[14] The desire of faculty in some disciplines to remain above the fray comes back to bite them when their disciplines come to be perceived by the public as useless, and therefore not an appropriate place to spend hard-earned tuition dollars. Today many scholars in philosophy, comparative literature, music, history, and many other disciplines are fully engaged in the world, modeling for their students the ways in which these fields of study can make important contributions to public life. Teaching philosophy in a prison, using music as a route to mathematics in underserved communities, historian-guided walks that surface the history of slavery or abolitionist activity in a community, reading Lolita in Tehran[15]—the ways in which knowledge-in-action from any discipline can create public good are endless. Just as we prepare doctors and lawyers for action in their fields, we should prepare all students with a discipline-infused sense of agency. When we educate for action, all subjects become "useful" subjects, and students are prepared to make their world, not simply to inherit it.

One of my greatest epiphanies as a teacher, mentioned briefly in Interlude E, came when I collaborated with a colleague in computer science. At the time, professor Fred Martin was doing a lot of work with simple electronic materials designed to be used by middle school teachers. These allowed students to take simple microprocessors and attach sensors and motors to create kinetic sculptures, interactive jewelry, and other fun projects. I was teaching an undergraduate general education course called "Sustainable Development," in which students learned about a variety of environmental challenges such as electronic waste, toxic chemicals in communities, urban sprawl, and recycling systems (this is the same course in which, a few years earlier, I had first tried Lego in class). Working with Martin, we introduced a hands-on project into the final three weeks of the class. For those three weeks, students worked in pairs in Martin's lab to respond to the challenge we gave them: "Create a model, device, or educational campaign linked to one or more of the topics of this course. Your device should in some way either a) take steps to solve a problem or issue from the course or b) assist in collecting data to better understand a problem or issue." Students built interactive models of a host of interesting devices, including a rover that could move through a field, sensing moisture and temperature and dropping a seed in places where the seed was most likely to sprout (these were all concept prototypes—we didn't expect students to build in three weeks devices robust enough to function outside the classroom). Another project modeled scanning product barcodes and displaying a score for that product reflecting its environmental friendliness and the quality of labor conditions in the factory where it was produced, anticipating by a few years apps like Good Guide and Buycott. Yet another attached a pH sensor to a remote-control model boat which could in theory be sent out into the Merrimack river near campus and map the contours of toxic spills.

I had a great time mentoring students as they worked on their projects, and being in the role of coach rather than Authority. The big revelation for me came a few days after the course ended, when I dropped into Fred's lab and found two of his student assistants there. They had both just completed the course, so I asked them what they thought of the project. Had they learned more about sustainable development from doing the project, or did they think they would have learned more if we had continued the format of the prior weeks of the course, with reading, discussion, videos, and the like. One of the students said: "I learned about sustainable development by doing the project, but what I *really* learned was that I could *do* something about it." It was an unforgettable moment for me. Students in past iterations of the course had asked for more information about solutions, so I had added a considerable amount of material about what activists and scientists were doing to improve sustainability. What I didn't realize is that my students, who were not from privileged backgrounds and were in many cases the first in their families to go to college, could not see themselves as people who could be future leaders in sustainability. It was not until we asked them to *do* something, to *make* something, and led them through a process of selecting a problem and figuring out what they could propose and model with the resources at hand, that they developed any sense of personal agency.

From that point on, I resolved to have a hands-on project in every course I possibly could. As an instructor, I had never been told about "project-based learning," but I was a convert to an approach I didn't know existed. Building student agency—educating for action—became my number one goal as I planned my classes. Memorization and retention of facts was secondary; what really mattered was building students' dispositions to act, and the habits of mind that would allow them to act intelligently in the world. Central to my effort has been teaching what is now loosely called *design thinking*, and an emphasis on student making in the classroom.

By stressing design and making as building blocks for student learning, I discovered much later that I was echoing John Dewey, who wrote that "Intelligent activity is distinguished from aimless activity by the fact that it involves selection of means—analysis—out of the variety of conditions that are present, and their arrangement—synthesis—to reach an intended aim or purpose."[16] So often in education we teach analysis, or perhaps critical thinking, without its necessary companion, synthesis. Critical thinking is an essential skill for students, and one we must continue to teach, but we must also guard against "analysis paralysis" by encouraging students to think of themselves as active agents, devising plans by synthesizing and arranging what they have understood into a purposeful plan of action.

In my class I emphasize synthesis more than analysis, because my students take a lot of courses which teach them analysis. Indeed, much of their education to this point has consisted of preparation for "knowing that" and for analysis. They are far less prepared for "knowing how," and for doing the synthetic work of design. In particular, as digital natives, I find that today's students understand less and less about the physical properties of the world and how to manipulate physical materials. A number of social and technological factors have combined to create in some students what Diane Levin calls "Problem Solving Deficit Disorder,"[17] which students develop through excessive exposure to situations in which they are not called upon to solve their own problems, but are given highly structured exercises, games, and settings in which they never have to confront the question of how to solve an open ended problem such as "I'm bored." The antidote to problem-solving deficit disorder is to be offered opportunities for synthesis, along with guidance from instructor, assignments, and available class materials to scaffold student learning and the development of a sense of agency.

Recommendation Four: Take Teaching and Learning Seriously

It should go without saying that teaching and learning would be the top priority in institutions of higher education, but sadly this is not always the case. Particularly in research universities like mine, the emphasis on research can eclipse teaching as a focus of effort and expenditure. Funding for research, patents, the prestige gained through faculty publications, and the expansion and maintenance of research facilities are often principal preoccupations of leadership in research universities. Liberal arts colleges and community colleges do not emphasize faculty research in the same way, so the teaching mission is central at these schools. Research is critically important, and student participation in research can be a life-changing experience, but when teaching comes to take a back seat to research, institutional priorities are out of whack.

At all colleges and universities, faculty professional development aimed at the continuous improvement of teaching should be a high priority, and given significant staff and resources. Many schools now have faculty development centers of some sort, and although these can vary in quality, level of support, and in the extent to which faculty use them, their very existence makes a statement about the value placed on teaching. Soon after I was hired as a new faculty member, my university created a faculty teaching center. The workshops I took there were a revelation, and introduced me to some of the literature on best practices in college teaching (before taking these workshops, I didn't even know there *was* research on learning in college, let alone what the findings were!).

I've come to think of it as a national scandal that college teachers do not need any training in how to teach, and can be ignorant, as I was, of what the research literature on college teaching says. Teachers in K-12 schools must, by law, have training in how to teach, but to teach grade 13 (our college freshmen) and beyond, no such instruction is required. In an institution devoted to learning, it goes against the grain to think that we ignore in our professional practice the guidance of research findings. Without exposure to research on learning, faculty tend to simply teach as they were taught, which risks perpetuating tired old practices that do a poor job of promoting student engagement and learning.

The great news is that I have seen faculty revitalized by new teaching practices and by the positive responses they engender in students. For me, a thinking-with-things approach, which evolved gradually over the course of my career, helped to keep my time in the classroom fresh and brought a welcome variety to familiar topics as students responded in their own ways to the challenges, big and small, that they encountered in my classroom. For a colleague in computer science, the transformation of his syllabus and his approach to each class meeting that resulted from his collaboration with an art professor was remarkable. Instead of giving all of his students identical assignments, and getting back student homework assignments that were mind-numbingly similar, his students implemented cell phone apps that reflected their interests and included the work of individual graphic design students with whom they were paired. Suddenly each student wanted to show their project to the others, and a collaborative spirit developed that inspired my colleague and revitalized his teaching. Improving teaching is a lot of effort for faculty, but it can be immensely rewarding as well.

I have seen faculty try a thinking-with-things approach in the classroom and express great happiness with the results. In many cases, these experiments become a regular part of the class when they teach it in future semesters. A colleague in mechanical engineering changed the material students in his "Materials Science for Engineers" class used to learn to test for shear stress (where adjacent parts of a material are forced in opposite directions) from a sheet of plastic to a colorful sample of machine-knitted textile. Students found the knitted fabric more engaging, and the change made the distortion of the material visible to the unaided eye. The change had the added effect that, because each team used a different type of knitted swatch, the test results were different for each group. Instead of just telling the students that they had gotten the right answer, my colleague now had to ask students for a description of their procedure. For students accustomed to finding a "right answer" in the textbook or from their professor, this was a novelty. Stretchy knits have become a staple of the class, replacing the standardized plastic sheeting.

In addition to emphasizing faculty development, the other major way in which institutions of higher education can truly take teaching and learning seriously is to examine and, if needed, revise the incentive structures within which faculty work. How does the school send the message that great pedagogy is truly valued and rewarded? Or conversely, what tells faculty that there are higher priorities than teaching, and that their success will depend on de-emphasizing instruction? When I was hired into my faculty position, there were colleagues who told me quite explicitly that I only had to be a good-enough teacher, and that my ability to get tenure would depend on my research and publications, not on the quality of my teaching. One even said "As long as your students are not staging sit-ins at the Chancellor's office to protest your teaching, you'll be okay." This was not, of course, the official position of the university, but apparently the actions of the institution up to that point had delivered a clear message to aspiring faculty about what was most valued. I have heard many similar stories from colleagues at other schools, so this was not a situation particular to the place I was working.

Although we faculty often don't like to think in these terms, higher education in the United States is a giant industry, and we are its employees. Like all employees, we work within a system that rewards some behaviors and discourages others. For institutions that truly value student learning and the development of essential life skills, a careful assessment of the quality of student learning and of the incentives for faculty to ensure strong student outcomes could help to identify what is and is not working to promote the development of our students. Many institutions already do some of this, but others accept half-measures or do only the minimum. Not to do this sends a message that student learning is not the top priority—an admission that should at least be acknowledged, if not challenged. As competitive pressure on the academy continues to increase, with rising costs of college attendance and the resulting crisis in student debt, investigating and documenting student learning becomes more critical. A thinking-with-things approach to student learning could not only improve outcomes; it could also become a selling point for residential, place-based colleges that are increasingly endangered. In a world where the digital is celebrated, on-campus learning can struggle to justify itself. Demonstrating the benefits of learning and thinking with things can help to show the value of supporting the embodied learner.

In this book I have tried to make a strong case for thinking with things, but in the long run there is no substitute for careful, detailed investigation of this approach to pedagogy. It is my fervent hope that I have persuaded my fellow faculty to explore what thinking with things, and a focus on supporting the embodied learner, can do to change their teaching and transform their classrooms. Along with this, I hope to inspire faculty and students to conduct in-depth research on what works, and why. (If you are in a field where you can achieve tenure and promotion by doing research on learning in your discipline, you can have the double reward of improving student learning and your prospects of promotion!) I am acutely aware that I have left the task of detailed research on the impact of thinking with things in the classroom to others, and I hope that what I have written will inspire their investigations. If only someone had written this book a generation ago, I could have stood on their shoulders. As it is, the book I was eager to read didn't exist, so I had to write it myself in order to be able to fully absorb its lessons.

Five Propositions

In Chapter 1, I presented the list of "Five Myths About Learning in College." I now offer "Five Propositions" to replace the myths I hope we can all surrender.

1. We think with our hands, our bodies, and our environments, not just with the contents of our craniums. "The life of the mind *is* the life of the body."
2. Thinking with Things promotes engagement, inquiry, insight, and emotion. It deepens learning and supports "knowing how" as well as "knowing that."
3. All learning is experiential, so it is critical to create classrooms and pedagogy that support the experiences that lead to knowledge and action.
4. The ability to grasp abstractions in a particular domain does not come automatically with age. Instead, it comes with the evolution from novice to expert, and this transition is aided by thinking with things.
5. By recognizing and supporting the embodied learner, we can abandon the sensory deprivation classroom and create learning environments that are enabling rather than disabling.

These five propositions, and the evidence from which they are derived, can guide us as we work to create a vibrant ecosystem for learning, in which our embodied students, and their teachers, will flourish.

Notes

1. Hilbert, D., & Cohn-Vossen, S. (1952/1999). *Geometry and the imagination* (P. Nemenyi, Trans., p. iii). Providence, RI: American Mathematical Society Chelsea Publishing, italics in the original.
2. Henderson, D. W., & Taimiņa, D. (2000). *Experiencing geometry*. New York, NY: Prentice Hall.
3. Beck, K., & Cunningham, W. (1989). A laboratory for teaching object oriented thinking. *ACM Sigplan Notices, 24*(10), 1–6. p. 4.
4. Beck, K., & Cunningham, W. (1989). A laboratory for teaching object oriented thinking. *ACM Sigplan Notices, 24*(10), 1–6. p. 5.
5. Walker, M., Takayama, L., & Landay, J. A. (2002, September). High-fidelity or low-fidelity, paper or computer? Choosing attributes when testing web prototypes. In *Proceedings of the human factors and ergonomics society annual meeting* (Vol. 46, No. 5, pp. 661–665). Los Angeles, CA: Sage Publications.
6. National Research Council, & Geographical Sciences Committee. (2005). *Learning to think spatially*. Washington, DC: National Academies Press.
7. Ritchhart, R., & Perkins, D. (2008). Making thinking visible. *Educational Leadership, 65*(5), 57. Retrieved from www.pz.harvard.edu/sites/default/files/makingthinkingvisibleEL.pdf
8. Dewey, J. (1938/1997). *Experience and education* (p. 40). New York, NY: Touchstone.
9. Duckworth, E. (2006). *The having of wonderful ideas and other essays on teaching and learning*. New York, NY: Teachers College Press.
10. Arnheim, R. (1969). *Visual thinking* (p. 3). Berkeley, CA: University of California Press.
11. Arnheim, R. (1969). *Visual thinking* (p. 296). Berkeley, CA: University of California Press.
12. Schön, D. A. (1983). *The reflective practitioner: How professionals think in action*. New York, NY: Basic Books.
13. Ryle, G. (2009). *The concept of mind*. New York, NY: Routledge.
14. Menand, L. (2010). *The marketplace of ideas* (p. 57). New York, NY: W. W. Norton & Company.
15. Nafisi, A. (2008). *Reading Lolita in Tehran: A memoir in books*. New York, NY: Random House.
16. Dewey, J. (1938/1997). *Experience and education* (p. 84). New York, NY: Touchstone.
17. Levin, D. E. (2007). Problem solving deficit disorder. *Paradigm Magazine*.

Index

Page numbers in *italics* indicate a figure.